UNEARTHING THE BIBLE

TITUS KENNEDY

HARVEST HOUSE PUBLISHERS
EUGENE, OREGON

Top photo on page 59 and photos on pages 146 and 234 are from Wikimedia. The Sphinx of Giza by Maison Bonfils, and John Rylands Papyrus by papyrologist Bernard Grenfell, courtesy of JRUL.

The James ossuary photos on pages 224 and 225 are © Paradiso and used with permission.

All other photos are © Titus Kennedy.

Cover design by Studio Gearbox

Cover photo © Infinity T29, Pakhnyushchy / Shutterstock

Unearthing the Bible
Copyright © 2020 by Titus Kennedy
Published by Harvest House Publishers
Eugene, Oregon 97408
www.harvesthousepublishers.com

ISBN 978-0-7369-7915-3 (pbk)
ISBN 978-0-7369-7916-0 (eBook)

Library of Congress Cataloging-in-Publication Data

Names: Kennedy, Titus Michael, author.
Title: Unearthing the Bible : 101 archaeological discoveries that bring the
    Bible to life / Titus Kennedy.
Description: Eugene : Harvest House Publishers, 2020. | Includes index. |
    Summary: "In Unearthing the Bible, Dr. Titus M. Kennedy presents 100
    objects from more than 50 museums, private collections, and
    archaeological sites, to offer strong and compelling evidence for the
    historical accuracy of Scripture"-- Provided by publisher.
Identifiers: LCCN 2019060224 (print) | LCCN 2019060225 (ebook) | ISBN
    9780736979153 (trade paperback) | ISBN 9780736979160 (ebook)
Subjects: LCSH: Bible--Antiquities. | Middle East--Antiquities.
Classification: LCC BS621 .K38 2020 (print) | LCC BS621 (ebook) | DDC
    220.9/3--dc23
LC record available at https://lccn.loc.gov/2019060224
LC ebook record available at https://lccn.loc.gov/2019060225

Printed in the United States of America

20 21 22 23 24 25 26 27 28 / VP-CD / 10 9 8 7 6 5 4 3 2 1

CONTENTS

CHAPTER 1 STORIES OF CREATION, FLOOD, BABEL, AND THE PATRIARCHS (Genesis and Job)

CHAPTER 2 THE ISRAELITES IN EGYPT, EXODUS, AND THE WILDERNESS (Exodus–Deuteronomy)

CHAPTER 3 CONQUEST, SETTLEMENT, AND THE JUDGES (Joshua–Ruth)

CHAPTER 4 THE UNITED MONARCHY OF SAUL, DAVID, AND SOLOMON (Samuel–Kings)

CHAPTER 5 SHATTERED KINGDOMS (Kings–Chronicles)

CHAPTER 6	**EMPIRES OF BABYLON AND PERSIA**
	(Jeremiah–Malachi)

CHAPTER 7	**JESUS AND HIS WORLD**
	(Matthew–John)

CHAPTER 8   THE FIRST CHRISTIANS AND THE
EARLY CHURCH (Acts–Revelation)

FOREWORD

I first became enchanted with biblical archaeology on a trip to Israel in 1989. During a walking tour in the old city of Jerusalem, a guide showed us some of the bullae or signet rings of Judahite officials that had been preserved since the Babylonian destruction of Jerusalem in 587 BC. The bullae bore the names of minor officials in the court of King Jehoiakim. I was fascinated by the detailed extrabiblical corroboration of specific events and biblical figures. I saw many more examples of such evidence during a month-long visit to Israel that year. That experience kindled in me what has become a lifelong fascination with such archaeological evidence.

During a sunny afternoon on an outdoor basketball court, I met Titus Kennedy. At the time, Titus was a senior in high school, and I was a young university professor teaching the philosophy of science. Titus distinguished himself on the court that day as he has done in nearly every facet of his life since. After the game, as the two of us stayed around and continued to shoot hoops, we struck up a conversation. Learning that he was going off to college, I asked him what major he planned to pursue. He told me he wanted to study archaeology and ancient history connected to the Bible. We soon discovered we had lots to discuss. As it turned out, I was teaching a course called "Reasons for Faith" that included a series of lectures on the evidence for the historical reliability of the Bible, primarily from archaeology.

Several years after this chance encounter, I reconnected with Titus. At the time, I was preparing to teach a filmed version of "Reasons for Faith" in front of a student audience for distribution as part of the TrueU series. By this time, Titus had finished a master's degree in Near Eastern archaeology from the University of Toronto. As a result of his studies, travels, and excavations, he had also acquired an expertise about the many archaeological artifacts connected to the historical narratives in the Bible. After hearing about the project, Titus agreed to review, fact check, and add to the archaeological content of my lectures. That turned out to be a good move on my part. It soon became apparent that Titus knew virtually everything there was to know about every known relevant artifact corroborating or otherwise illuminating the biblical narrative. During this preparation, I also learned that Titus possessed a rare commitment to both scientific rigor and biblical authority. A few years later, Titus received his doctorate in biblical archaeology from the University of South Africa for his work on the demography of Canaan during the period of Moses, Joshua, and the judges. We also taught a memorable summer course together in Cambridge, England, capped with an unforgettable tour led by Titus through the British Museum. Over those hours in the museum, biblical history came to life for our students.

Based on my experience working so closely with Titus on these and other projects, I can highly recommend this book. Many in our elite media and academic culture reflexively reject the biblical message as factually and historically inaccurate, thinking that surely the relevant archaeological evidence supports such a judgment. This book instead shows that a surprising array of evidence supports the historical reliability of the biblical text, and does so across different periods of biblical history, from the time of Abraham to that of Moses, Joshua, David, Hezekiah, Daniel, Jesus, and Paul.

In documenting and displaying these objects, Dr. Kennedy provides information about where they were found and when they were created—what archaeologists call provenancing and dating. He also provides important insight into their interpretation and relevance to understanding the biblical text. His beautiful photographs of these artifacts also help bring them, and the events to which they attest, to life. The pictures and articles in this book will ignite the same kind of interest for many readers. Many will also find this volume a helpful aid in their own Bible study. Think of it as a kind of archaeological commentary on historical narratives in the biblical books.

Titus Kennedy is a dedicated archaeologist who has traveled to difficult locations, slept with scorpions, and lowered himself into excavation shafts to document critical archaeological evidence supporting the Bible. No one else I know combines such a fearless spirit of adventure, love of the Bible, knowledge of ancient languages, careful scholarship, and archaeological expertise. Having part of this knowledge under one cover, illustrated with color photographs, makes this book a treasure. Read, view, and enjoy!

Stephen C. Meyer, PhD
Discovery Institute

INTRODUCTION

Artifacts left behind from the vanished, ancient world of the Bible have been found and recovered through archaeology. What is an artifact? In simple terms, an artifact is an ancient object made or modified by humans, and many have been found, especially in recent years, at archaeological sites around the world. Artifacts include statues, altars, jewelry, weapons, tools, inscriptions, paintings, coins, scarabs, tablets, papyri, stelae, reliefs, and pottery, showcasing the artistic and technological prowess of the ancients. But more importantly, artifacts tell stories of the past. They serve as both visual and informational aids that provide insight into that ancient context and toward an accurate understanding and interpretation.

The Bible is a collection of books written millennia ago in places and cultures far removed from modern readers, but artifacts can give us essential knowledge of the ancient world and help us avoid the problem of unconsciously or inadvertently viewing a passage or book in the context of a modern society and time.

Because the Bible contains stories from the ancient world, written in a style different than the method of modern historians and paired with theology, many have assumed that the narratives in the Bible are myth, legend, and propaganda instead of accurate history. In fact, the majority of scholars, most media and educational sources, and many in the general public regard the Bible as a fairy tale and frequently portray it as unimportant or irrelevant beyond literary and religious studies. For years, the Bible has been routinely attacked and disregarded on the basis of history or archaeology.

And yet when people look into what archaeologists have unearthed, a different story comes to light, showing that instead of fiction and fairy tales, archaeology indicates that the Bible preserves an accurate recounting of the history addressed in its pages. Specifically, hundreds of artifacts from the distant past have demonstrated the events, people, and places in the Bible to be historical.

The goal of this book is twofold—to provide a resource with quality photographs and information about archaeological artifacts that illuminate the story and context of the Bible for a more thorough and accurate understanding of the Scriptures, and to demonstrate how artifacts also confirm the historical reliability of passages in the Bible.

I have been interested in history and art as long as I can remember, and walking through museums and seeing archaeological artifacts always gives me a sense of mystery, admiration, and wonder. These remnants of a culture or person from so many centuries ago, often long forgotten, can preserve and communicate important information and ideas beyond the written word of a history book, and add dimension and depth to the ancient writings.

And that is why I have written this book. Over the years, I have done research and photography of archaeological artifacts in museums, private collections, and archaeological sites around the world. I am a professional field archaeologist who holds a doctorate and two master's degrees in biblical archaeology and Near Eastern archaeology, specializing in biblical archaeology of both the Old Testament and New Testament. My background in archaeology, ancient history, Bible, and artifacts has given me rather unique qualifications for writing a book on this topic.

My hope is that this book will fill a niche by providing high-quality photographs of over 100 of the most important artifacts connected to the Bible, along with thorough and accurate information and interpretation, presented in a logical and accessible format for the general reader, the student, and the scholar. To accomplish this task, the book includes high-resolution color photographs, has been organized chronologically by historical periods and books of the Bible, and contains descriptions and explanations for each artifact along with biblical references.

CHAPTER 1

STORIES OF CREATION, FLOOD, BABEL, AND THE PATRIARCHS

(Genesis and Job)

Prior to the many discoveries and analyses now available to modern archaeologists and historians, skeptical scholars claimed that Genesis and the Pentateuch were composed from four basic sources written during the Israelite Monarchy period from the 10th to 6th century BC, that Genesis had merely copied the Mesopotamian stories of creation and the flood with minor monotheistic variation, and that the lives of the patriarchs were myths that did not accurately reflect their alleged historical period. Subsequent discoveries and research, however, threw this documentary hypothesis into disarray and forced alternative explanations. Further, it has become apparent that the Genesis creation narrative was not merely a copy of another polytheistic creation story, and that the patriarchs accurately reflect the historical period in which they are set.

The narratives in the book of Genesis cover the major events of creation of the world and humans, the Great Flood, the Tower of Babel, establishment of the earliest nations, and then a shift to the lives of Abraham, Isaac, Jacob, Joseph, and their families. Beginning with the life story of Abraham, these biographical sections of Genesis focus on one family over the course of nearly 400 years in the regions of Mesopotamia, Canaan, and Egypt during an archaeological period known as the Middle Bronze Age (ca. 2000–1500 BC).

The setting for the book of Job is likewise in the Middle Bronze Age and probably around the time of Abraham or Isaac, indicated by the lack of reference to Israel or the Law of Moses, Job functioning as the priest of his family (Job 1:5), the lifetime of Job recorded as over 140 years (Job 42:16), and certain social customs and names best fitting this time period.

The artifacts presented in this section originate primarily from Mesopotamia and Egypt, span nearly 1,500 years, and include written records about events, places, people, laws, and customs, in addition to important artistic depictions from the period.

(1) ALTERNATE CREATION TABLETS
(Girsu and Ebla)

Date: 3rd millennium BC

Discovered: Girsu (Tell Telloh, Iraq) and Ebla (Tell Mardikh, Syria)

Period: Genesis 1–11

Keywords: creation; Mesopotamia; tablet; Girsu; Ebla

Bible Passages: Genesis 1:1–2:1; Job 38:4-7; Psalm 148:1-5; Colossians 1:15-16

The Sumerians, who composed the oldest written records of any civilization yet discovered, wrote about the origins of the heavens and earth through a story of creation. A Sumerian cuneiform[1] clay tablet[2] discovered at Girsu in southern Mesopotamia and composed during the Early Dynastic period in the 3rd millennium BC, perhaps as early as 2900 BC, recounts a time at the beginning of creation in which the daylight and moonlight did not shine because the sun and moon did not yet exist, the "lesser gods" had not yet been created, the fields and vegetation were still merely dust, and the earth was filled with water as part of the creation process.

This text also mentions heaven, earth, and water, which were often personified as the original divine trio in ancient Mesopotamian creation stories, although Lord

---

[1] *Cuneiform:* A wedge-shaped form of writing invented by the Sumerians that was simplified from the pictographic writing system that preceded it. It was used to write numerous languages, including Sumerian, Akkadian, Hittite, and Eblaite.

[2] *Tablet:* The clay tablets commonly used during the Bronze Age in the Ancient Near East were typically rectangular in shape and the written text was impressed into the wet clay with a reed stylus. Some tablets were baked, others were dried, but many of the preserved tablets discovered by archaeologists underwent an unintentional hardening process when a building that housed tablets was destroyed by fire.

Heaven is specifically referred to in the narrative—perhaps as the creator. This tablet, which might be the oldest preserved creation story, has obvious parallels to the Genesis account as it refers to a beginning, then the creation of the sun, moon, water on the earth, and vegetation. The "lesser gods" in ancient Near Eastern literature appear to be angelic beings, which according to the Bible seem to have been created before the earth, and the concept of the Trinity even appears to be implied in the Genesis creation narrative.

Another one of the most ancient creation accounts was discovered in a cache of about 20,000 clay tablets during excavations at Ebla, Syria (Tell[3] Mardikh) in northern Mesopotamia. More than 8,000 of these tablets at Ebla were from a city archive dated to about 2400–2000 BC, prior to a destruction of the city. Texts were written in the scripts of both Sumerian and Akkadian[4], but a local Eblaite dialect was discovered in the documents. Out of these thousands of tablets, three that contain a short creation poem have been recovered and translated. The texts are in the Eblaite language and contain one of the oldest known creation accounts.

The poem states, "Lord of heaven and earth, you had not made the earth exist, you created. You had not established the sun, you created. You had not made the morning light exist." It also notes that this Lord is divine, saves, and has words that produce effects. The recovered fragments of the poem are concerned primarily with the initial creation of earth, light, and the sun, while sections such as the creation of plants, animals, and humans were either not addressed or may have been in lost sections of the poem.

The Girsu creation tablet and the Eblaite creation hymn, which share more similarities to the beginning of Genesis than any other known ancient creation texts, are also the oldest copies of creation accounts yet discovered. While these Mesopotamian creation texts are not exactly the same as Genesis or other related creation passages in the Bible, especially regarding clear monotheism, order, and comprehensiveness, they do demonstrate remembrance and knowledge of a very similar creation idea throughout the ancient Near East very early in the history of civilization.

> *In the beginning God created the heavens and the earth. The earth was formless and void, and darkness was over the surface of the deep, and the Spirit of God was hovering over the surface of the waters. Then God said, "Let there be light" and there was light (Genesis 1:1-3).*

---

[3] *Tell* or *Tel:* A mound consisting of debris and ruins from ancient cities or towns built on top of one another at the same archaeological site. In certain situations, the mound was formed purposefully in order to create an artificial hill.

[4] *Akkadian:* Refers to the Akkadian language of Mesopotamia, the oldest known Semitic language, or to the empire or people from the Akkadian Empire, founded by Sargon of Akkad in the 24th century BC.

(2) THE DOUBLE CREATION OF HUMANS
(Enuma Elish, Enki and Ninhursag, Adapa)

Date: 2nd millennium BC

Discovered: Nineveh, Iraq

Period: Genesis 1–11

Keywords: creation; Adam; Eve; humans; Eden; angels

Bible Passage: Genesis 1:26–3:24

The first words of the Babylonian creation epic Enuma Elish mean "when on high" and refer to the abode of the original gods before the earth had been created and named. Currently, the earliest known copies date to about 1000 BC from Babylon, but the poem was possibly composed in the Old Babylonian period around 1700 BC based on context and linguistics. Enuma Elish was first rediscovered in the library of Ashurbanipal at Nineveh, but subsequent copies have been recovered since.

The story emphasizes how Marduk[5] was elevated to the chief god of the pantheon in the context of creation and a struggle between the gods, and that Babylon should be regarded as supreme. Three primeval gods exist at the beginning: Abzu (fresh water), Tiamat (salt water), and Mummu (the mist), and the text is divided into seven sections, with the creation of man in section 6 and the recitation of the names and titles of Marduk in section 7. The sevenfold division with the creation

---

[5] *Marduk:* Patron god of Babylon and chief god of the pantheon by the 18th century BC. Marduk was also referred to by the title Bel. He was associated with the dragon.

of man in the sixth and honoring the god Marduk in the seventh has been compared to Genesis and the days of creation, with Adam on the sixth day, followed by the seventh day of rest.

Enuma Elish narrates the separation of heavens and earth as Tiamat is slain and split in two, the "lesser gods" are created (perhaps equivalent to angelic beings), man is created, and after this Babylon is constructed and a ziggurat[6] temple is built for Marduk. Parallels with the Genesis narrative can be seen, such as the "original creator gods" existing before creation, the separation of the heavens and earth, creation of angelic beings, creation of man, resting of the gods, and building of cities.

Mankind, whose purpose according to the story was to work so that the gods may rest, was created utilizing divine blood from a sacrificed god named Kingu. In the Atra-Hasis creation of man section, it is specified that man was created by shaping him from clay and combining that with the divine blood, similar to what is recorded in Genesis when God shaped Adam from the dust of the earth and breathed the divine breath of life into him.

The Sumerian epic Enki and Ninhursag also addresses the creation of man. In this account, clay is fashioned into the first man who is brought into existence, followed by five additional humans, and each are appointed a job to do.

An ancient Sumerian text addressing the life of a man after creation, a story called Adapa after the name of the protagonist, is set in the early days of antediluvian[7] (preflood) Mesopotamia, recounts events in the life of the model man or human archetype. The earliest known text of this story was discovered at Amarna and dates to about the 14th century BC, but the story was obviously

---

[6] *Ziggurat:* A monumental structure of successively terraced platforms constructed with clay bricks. A ziggurat was associated with religion, usually had a shrine or temple at the top, and may have been seen as a connection between earth and the heavens. The Etemenanki ziggurat in Babylon, now in ruins, was approximately 300 feet tall (91 meters), but larger ziggurats may have existed previously.

[7] *Antediluvian:* Before the great flood.

composed much earlier, and ritual incantations found at Nippur from as early as 1800 BC invoke the name Adapa, who was known from Sumerian sources as the first of the antediluvian sages.

Some linguists have suggested Adapa could be rendered Adamu or may at least share the same original word root with Adam. In the story, this model man talked with the gods, underwent a test from the gods involving the food of life and water of life in the realm of the gods, was judged by another god for his refusal to eat what was offered, and finally was sent back to earth without eternal life and with the penalty of disease on humanity.[8] The connection of Adapa to Adam due to linguistics, events, and themes has been debated, but the similarities are noteworthy.

That multiple ancient Mesopotamia stories record the creation of man by shaping him from clay and infusing him with divine blood, extremely similar to the Genesis account of shaping man from dust and infusing him with divine breath, indicates that knowledge of the creation of man story had been passed down from centuries before, perhaps in both oral and written form, and adapted to suit the various gods and theologies.

> *Then Yahweh God formed man of dust from the ground, and breathed into his nostrils the breath of life, and man became a living being (Genesis 2:7).*

---

[8] This test or temptation of Adam and Eve may also be illustrated on a seal from 2200 BC found in Mesopotamia. The stone seal depicts a male and a female sitting on either side of a sacred tree, with a serpent behind the female. When the seal was discovered, scholars immediately noticed the possible parallel, although in modern times ideas about the seal have been distanced from Adam and Eve in the Garden of Eden.

(3) The Mesopotamian Version of the Flood
(Atra-Hasis)

Date: 1900 BC

Discovered: Unknown, Iraq

Period: Genesis 1–11

Keywords: Atra-Hasis; flood; Noah; Gilgamesh; Utnapishtum; Ziusudra

Bible Passages: Genesis 6:5–8:22; 2 Peter 2:5

Atra-Hasis, meaning "exceedingly wise," is the title of an ancient Akkadian epic derived from the name of the protagonist. The epic, which contains narratives about creation and the flood, has been of particular interest due to its detailed ancient flood story and its similarity to the Noah narrative.

Recently, a tablet written about 1900 BC and sourced from a private collection was rediscovered and translated, containing the flood story of Atra-Hasis, who interacts with the god Enki. Measuring 11.5 cm by 6 cm, it contains 60 lines of cuneiform. In this particular text, many specifics were noticed that match the flood story of Noah found in Genesis: gods want to destroy all humans by a flood; one god warns a man about the flood and instructs him to build a boat; dimensions are given for a massive boat to be built with bitumen, multiple decks, and a roof; animals were taken on board two by two; a storm rages and the world floods;

the boat lands on a mountain; and the survivor offers a sacrifice to the god who saved him.

While many similarities are obvious, notable differences also exist, such as multiple gods rather than one God; the flood was sent as a result of overpopulation and noise annoying the gods instead of sin corrupting the earth; craftsmen of the city help Atra-Hasis construct the boat; it rains for 7 days instead of 40; the sacrifice is eaten by the gods; and the dimensions of the boat—rounded with an approximate 70 meter diameter and 6 meter high walls—are slightly different.

Tablet 11 of the Epic of Gilgamesh contains the flood story as told by Utnapishtim, who appears to be the same person as Atra-Hasis. The Gilgamesh version of the story about a man building a boat to survive a divinely sent flood that wipes out mankind goes back to ca. 2100 BC in Sumerian texts, and all of the earliest flood accounts, including Atra-Hasis, Gilgamesh, and Ziusudra, appear to descend from a common source.

Although the Genesis account is unique in its monotheistic perspective and discussion of sin, the Mesopotamian texts, along with several others from the ancient world, such as the Deucalion version in Greek, undoubtedly recount the same basic story.

> *Behold, I, even I am bringing the flood of water upon the earth, to destroy all flesh in which is the breath of life, from under heaven; everything that is on the earth shall perish...you shall enter the ark...And of every living thing of all flesh, you shall bring two of every kind into the ark, to keep them alive with you (Genesis 6:17-19).*

(4) The Preflood World
(Sumerian King List)

Date: 2000 BC
Discovered: Larsa, Iraq
Period: Genesis 1–11
Keywords: Sumerian; antediluvian; flood
Bible Passage: Genesis 5:3–10:10

The Sumerian King List preserves a record of the kings of Sumer from local and foreign dynasties, including reign lengths and brief supplemental historical information. The oldest known sources preserving this list are a tablet from Larsa dating to about 2000 BC (WB 62) and the Weld-Blundell Prism (WB 444) from slightly before 1800 BC as it ends with a king named Sin-magir of Isin who reigned in the late 19th century BC. The four-sided prism[9] measures about 7.9 inches tall (20 cm) and 3.5 inches wide (9 cm), and the clay was impressed with cuneiform in the Sumerian language.

These cuneiform texts of the Sumerian King List are unique in that they record the names and extremely long reigns of the kings before the great deluge, the first city where kings ruled, and a brief mention of the flood. The reigns of these antediluvian kings were measured in the Sumerian numerical units known as sars

---

[9] *Prism:* In archaeology, a prism typically refers to a four-sided clay artifact that usually contains writing on each of the sides.

(3,600), ners (600), and sosses (60) since the Sumerians operated with a sexagesimal base 60 mathematical system instead of the base 10 system commonly used today.

The text begins with "After the kingship descended from heaven, the kingship was in Eridu…" and goes on to list eight preflood rulers with incredibly long lifespans ranging from 18,600 to 43,200 units. Archaeologically, Eridu at Tell Abu Shahrain has been considered the oldest city in Mesopotamia and possibly the oldest city in the world. It has also been suggested as the location of the Tower of Babel due to its possible status as the "first city" and a massive, ancient ziggurat constructed there.

Following the list of these eight kings, the text then mentions "after the flood swept over…the kingship was in Kish" before continuing the record of later dynasties and kings. This city of Kish was probably founded around 3100 BC. Perhaps it is coincidence, but after Adam, there are also eight men listed in Genesis before Noah and the flood.

Although the long reigns in the Sumerian King List probably do not correspond to our calculation of years, or the numbers are drastically inflated, comparison between the preflood and postflood reigns demonstrates that the Sumerians believed that the preflood kings had lifespans several times longer than those who lived after the flood, similar to a comparison between preflood and postflood lifespans in Genesis.

As such, the Weld-Blundell Prism and the tablet from Larsa are ancient Mesopotamian sources up to 600 years before Moses that document widespread belief that Eridu was the first city, people before the flood had extremely long lifespans, and a flood reset civilization prior to 3000 BC.

> *Now Noah was six hundred years old when the flood of water came upon the earth (Genesis 7:6).*

(5) THE TOWER OF BABEL
(Enmerkar and the Lord of Aratta)

Date: 2000 BC

Discovered: Nippur; Ur; Kish

Period: Genesis 1–11

Keywords: Enmerkar; Uruk; ziggurat; Babel; Tower of Babel; Shinar; Sumer

Bible Passage: Genesis 10:8–11:9

The ancient Sumerian story of Enmerkar and the Lord of Aratta was composed prior to 2000 BC and focuses on Enmerkar, king of Uruk, and his conflicts with the unnamed king of Aratta. According to the Sumerian King List, Enmerkar probably ruled around 2600 BC or earlier, making him one of the earliest known kings. In the Sumerian epic about Enmerkar, who was recorded as the founder of the city of Uruk, he attempted to build the E-Abzu temple in the city of Eridu.[10]

The text is a composite from 27 currently known tablets and fragments discovered in at least 3 different locations in Mesopotamia. Archaeologically, Eridu is often considered the earliest known city in the world, and the E-Abzu temple ziggurat is the largest and oldest known, yet it was also unfinished.

Based on Sumerian architecture and the method in which the largest tower temples and monuments were built in the ancient world, the Tower of Babel was probably a massive ziggurat. These ziggurats were designed as large stepped-platform structures made from fired clay bricks and constructed with a temple at the top as a house for the gods of heaven or as a link between heaven and earth.

In Enmerkar and the Lord of Aratta, the ruler Enmerkar attempts to construct

---

[10] References to the land of Shinar/Sumer and early Mesopotamian cities such as Uruk and Akkad in the Tower of Babel narrative suggest that it accurately reflects an extremely ancient time when the Sumerian civilization was first established.

a gigantic ziggurat. The building they are constructing is variously called "a holy mountain," "a temple brought down from heaven," "a great shrine," and "an abode of the gods," indicating both its size and its function. Then, an incantation is sung that all the people may address the god Enlil in a single language, and the text states that the god Enki will change the speech in their mouths so the speech of mankind is truly one.

This Sumerian epic appears to reflect knowledge of the Tower of Babel story, specifically with the building of a massive tower temple reaching toward the heavens in one of the first cities of Mesopotamia, a direct connection to the city of Erech/Uruk, and the reference to a single language of humanity that came about as an act of divine intervention.

However, the Enmerkar story seems to be a partial reversal of the Genesis account—one of the gods changing the many languages back to one language as it was before the building of the Tower of Babel, and no record of the failure to complete the tower temple or of the dispersion of the people in rebellion.

A section of the story reads as "the whole universe…may they all address Enlil together in a single language! For at that time…Enki…shall change the speech in their mouths, as many as he had placed there, and so the speech of mankind is truly one."

Found in the writings of Josephus, the Tower of Babel had been attributed to Nimrod in antiquity because he established Babel, and a few scholars have even suggested a connection between Nimrod and Enmerkar because both were kings, ruled over Erech/Uruk, and both have an association with a massive tower or ziggurat and the changing of human speech through divine intervention. Although the timelines and all of the details may not match exactly, the story of Enmerkar and the Lord of Aratta does appear to include knowledge of the Tower of Babel event, although in an alternate version.

> *The beginning of [Nimrod's] kingdom was Babel and Erech and Accad and Calneh, in the land of Shinar…*
>
> *Now the whole earth used the same language and the same words…they used brick for stone, and they used tar for mortar. They said, "Come, let us build for ourselves a city, and a tower whose top will reach into heaven…" The Lord said… "Come, let Us go down and there confuse their language, so that they will not understand one another's speech" (Genesis 10:10; 11:1-7).*

(6) ABRAHAM AND UR
(Lament for Ur)

Date: 1950 BC
Discovered: Ur; Nippur
Period: Patriarchs
Keywords: Ur; Abram; Abraham; Terah; Elamites
Bible Passage: Genesis 11:31–12:5

The Lament for the Destruction of Ur is a Mesopotamian poem consisting of 438 lines divided into 11 sections and is known from several tablets discovered at Nippur, Ur, and other ancient cities of Mesopotamia. The most exceptional of these tablets measures 24.5 cm by 13.6 cm and has been preserved nearly intact over the millennia. Composed by an unknown author, the document recorded and lamented the destruction of Ur by the Elamites and their allies during the final year of King Ibbi-Sin of the 3rd Dynasty of Ur around 1950 BC.

Written from a Sumerian perspective, the text mentions several deities discussing the end of Ur III, with Ningal pleading, ineffectively, before a divine council to spare Ur. Fortifications had been built around the city, but the defenses did not prevent the onslaught of the Elamites. In graphic poetic language, the verses describe how the city was reduced to ruin, temples were destroyed, corpses were piled at the gates, severed heads were scattered on the streets, bodies decomposed in the sun, families were burned in their houses, people died of hunger, treasures were defiled and stolen, and those who survived groaned in lamentation.

Since Ur was probably the largest city in the world at the time, with a population of at least 65,000, the event significantly changed the history and demography of the region. Following the destruction of Ur, the city eventually came under the control of a dynasty based in Larsa. Although a violent military siege ended Ur, the decline of the empire had begun earlier due to economic and political factors.

Leading up to these events in the Genesis account, Abram was probably living in the city, and the departure of the family of Terah, including Abram and Sarai, may have coincided with the campaign of the Elamites around 1950 BC. Prior to the siege of the city, when the empire was already floundering, Terah may have thought it advisable to leave. If the disintegrating political and economic situation did not convince them to leave, surely the impending attack upon the city would have. Whatever prompted his decision, Terah moved his family north from Ur to Haran, where Abram lived for about 50 years before migrating to Canaan.

> Terah took Abram his son, and Lot the son of Haran, his grandson, and Sarai his daughter-in-law, his son Abram's wife; and they went out together from Ur of the Chaldeans in order to enter the land of Canaan; and they went as far as Haran, and settled there (Genesis 11:31).

(7) DESECRATION OF NAMES
(Execration Texts)

Date: 2000–1800 BC

Discovered: Saqqara, Egypt

Period: Patriarchs

Keywords: Abraham; Zebulun; Job; Jacob; Laish; Shechem; Salem

Bible Passages: Genesis 12:6–14:18; 33:18; 35:23-29; Job 1:1

The Egyptian Execration Texts, which were essentially ceremonial curse texts, are known from the 6th Dynasty through the New Kingdom (ca. 2345–1077 BC). The texts, consisting primarily of the names of enemies of Egypt, including cities and personal names, were typically written on statuettes, bowls, and tablets that were shattered. The ritual of breaking these texts with the names of enemies and then burying them was a type of sympathetic magic intended to curse and destroy the people and places written on the texts.

Clay figurines or statuettes shaped as humans with the enemy names written in black or red ink were the most common form of Egyptian execration texts. Over 1,000 of the figurines and bowls have been excavated throughout Egypt, demonstrating how common the practice was over a period of several centuries.

The ceremony involved crafting the curse object and writing the names of enemies upon it, smashing the object, then destroying and desecrating it with other methods such as spitting, trampling with the left foot, stabbing with a spear and a knife, placing the object in a fire, and finally burying the pieces. At a few sites, evidence of the execration ritual was even discovered in conjunction with human and animal sacrifice, such as at Avaris in the 18th Dynasty, including severed heads, fingers, and the remains of two men.

During the Middle Kingdom this practice was especially prolific, and the Execration Texts are an important source of information about the names of cities and personal names in use in the Canaan region. Excavations at Saqqara uncovered many of the broken figurines that named more than 60 cities, tribes, and people in Canaan during the Middle Bronze Age from about 2000–1700 BC. Many of the names of cities and people mentioned in these texts are also found in the book of Genesis narratives set in the Middle Bronze Age, including Laish, Shechem, Jerusalem (Salem), Abraham (Aburahana), Zebulun, and even Job. Abram visited Salem (Jerusalem), Shechem, and Laish (Dan), while Jacob visited Shechem.

Several other ancient texts and inscriptions from the Middle Bronze Age also mention names found in the patriarchal narratives of Genesis. For example, three cuneiform tablets from about 1965 BC found at the ancient Mesopotamian city of Dilbat, an area on the Euphrates south of Babylon and north of Ur, mention a man named Abarama son of Awel-Ishtar. These tablets show the use of the name Abram in southern Mesopotamia precisely at the time of Abram son of Terah, who originated in Ur according to the book of Genesis.

Many scarabs from Egypt and Canaan dated to the Middle Bronze Age have also been found inscribed with the name Yaqob or Jacob, and this type of "Amorite Imperfective" name, which was common during the period, is expressed in the names Isaac, Jacob, and Joseph.

The use and popularity of personal names constantly changed over time in the ancient world, meaning that certain names were usually restricted to a particular time period and even region. While city names often stayed the same for century or millennia if people continued to live there, in certain cases the names would be changed or modified, such as Salem to Jerusalem and Laish to Dan. Therefore, several personal names in Genesis that are known archaeologically from Middle Bronze Age sources, combined with place names that changed after that period, suggest that the stories about Abraham, Isaac, Jacob, Job, Zebulun, and others are situated historically in the period of approximately 2000–1600 BC.

Abram passed through the land as far as the site of Shechem (Genesis 12:6).

(8) LAWS, CUSTOMS, ECONOMY, AND HAMMURABI
(Stele of Hammurabi)

Date: 1750 BC

Discovered: Susa (originally from Sippar)

Period: Patriarchs

Keywords: Hammurabi; law; customs; Abraham; Reuben; Joseph

Bible Passages: Genesis 21:1-10; 35:22; 37:23-28; 49:1-4; 1 Chronicles 5:1

The Stele of Hammurabi, carved from basalt and standing 2.25 meters (7.5 feet) tall, was inscribed with 282 laws in Old Akkadian from the famous 18th-century BC Code of Hammurabi. It was found during excavations at ancient Susa, but the stele[11] was probably transported from its original location in Sippar to the place of its discovery in Susa by the Elamites in the 12th century BC.

The image at the top of the stele shows the sun god Shamash, associated with justice, seated on a throne, and Hammurabi king of Babylon standing in front of him. According to the epilogue, anyone could come to read the stele, and it was probably erected in a public area.

Composed around 1750 BC, the code contains information from the era about contracts, social customs, punishments, and economics. Since the code is from the approximate time of Jacob and Joseph, the laws, customs, and prices found in the code reflect information and customs from that period that are also found in

---

[11] *Stele:* A monument stone or wooden slab erected for commemorative purposes, usually inscribed with writing and decoration, and occasionally painted.

the book of Genesis, such as premier status being given to the son of the first wife regardless of birth order, or the loss of birthright due to offense against the family.

Laws 170 and 171 state to give the inheritance portion to the son of the first wife, not the son of the female slave, which is also reflected in Genesis when Isaac was made the heir because he was born of Sarah, even though Ishmael had been chronologically the firstborn son but was born to Hagar the slave.

Many years later, Reuben lost his firstborn birthrights due to the serious offense against the family of defiling his father's bed. In the Code of Hammurabi, laws 158, 168, and 169 contain rules and customs about loss of the birthright due to this same serious offense against the family.

When Joseph was sold into slavery to Ishmaelite traders only decades after the reign of Hammurabi, his purchase price was shekels, which is also the exact value of a slave stated by the Code of Hammurabi in laws 116, 214, and 252. Earlier law codes state lower prices, such as that of Ur Nammu in about 2050 BC where the value of a slave was 10 shekels, then 15 shekels in the Laws of Eshnunna about 1930 BC. Prices continued to increase, and after the time of Hammurabi we find examples of 30 shekels at Ugarit in the 14th century BC and 50 shekels in Assyria during the 8th century BC.

The data shows that prices differed according to time period, and the Code of Hammurabi demonstrates that the slave price of 20 shekels paid for Joseph and recorded in Genesis coincides with the approximate time of Hammurabi in the 18th century BC, which is also the date determined for Joseph using chronological information found in the Bible.

The laws, customs, and prices found in the Code of Hammurabi from the 18th century BC in the Middle Bronze Age and the patriarchal narratives from the time of Isaac, Jacob, and Joseph in Genesis suggest that the events occurred in the same period and accurately reflect conditions of that specific time.

Then some Midianite traders passed by, so they pulled him up and lifted Joseph out of the pit, and sold him to the Ishmaelites for twenty shekels of silver (Genesis 37:28).

(9) Names, Covenants, and Social Customs
(Mari and Nuzi Tablets)

Date: 18th and 16th century BC

Discovered: Mari (Tell Hariri, Syria) and Nuzi (Yorghan Tepe, Iraq)

Period: Patriarchs

Keywords: Mari; Nuzi; Horite; customs; covenant; adoption; birthright; teraphim; Abraham; Haran; Laish

Bible Passages: Genesis 11:31–12:4; 14:7-14; 15:2-18; 16:1-2; 20:12; 25:27-34; 27:1-4; 29:1-30; 30:1-13; 31:14-19; 48:1-9; Leviticus 18:6-18; 20:7; 2 Kings 23:24

At ancient Mari in northern Mesopotamia, a huge archive of about 25,000 Akkadian cuneiform tablets from the Middle Bronze Age was discovered within the palace complex during excavations, most from the 18th century BC, and many specifically from the reign of the Amorite king Zimrilim around 1760 BC.[12] The tablets include references to various customs and names unique to the period. The city was a major center of the Amorite people who were prominent in the region from about 2000–1600 BC—

---

[12] The site of ancient Mari is located in northern Syria, near the homeland of the biblical patriarchs, about 200 miles (320 km) SE of Haran. The first tablets at Mari were discovered in 1933.

the time of Abraham, Isaac, Jacob, and Joseph.[13]

The Amorites, many of whom were originally nomadic, had lived in Canaan and northern Mesopotamia, eventually growing more powerful and becoming a dominant force centered at Mari by about 1800 BC. However, just after 1600 BC they began to be assimilated into newly emerging empires, and by the 14th century BC had nearly disappeared.

The Amorites are mentioned in Genesis during the time of Abraham and Jacob, who had personal interactions with them. Some of the tablets found at Mari even describe a covenant practice that was recorded in Genesis during the life of Abraham—specifically utilizing animal slaughter when a land covenant is made to show the solemnity of the covenant.

In these tablets from the 18th century BC found at Mari, many personal names match or are similar to those recorded in Genesis during the time of the patriarchs, including Abram, Laban, Jacob, and Mare-Yamina, which appears similar to Benjamin. While these are not attestations of the individuals written about in Genesis, it does demonstrate that those names were in use during the Middle Bronze Age in Mesopotamia.

Two important cities from the patriarchal narratives are also mentioned in the Mari archive—Haran, one of the cities where Abraham lived, and Laish (later named Dan), which Abraham visited as he journeyed to settle in Canaan. The discoveries at Mari of the same specific land-grant covenant form, in addition to personal and place names of the time and region, suggest that the narratives about the patriarchs in Genesis accurately reflect the historical period in which they are set.

Tablets from an archive discovered at Nuzi, a prominent ancient city near the Tigris River in northern Mesopotamia, were written mostly in Hurrian (Horite) and date from about 1500 BC.[14] Examination of these tablets revealed that many social and cultural customs documented at Nuzi show a match between customs

---

[13] Because Akkadian was the most prominent Semitic language spoken and written in ancient Mesopotamia, it was probably the native language of Abraham in Ur.

[14] About 5,000 tablets are currently known from Nuzi. Some of the tablets discovered at Mari are Akkadian and date from around 2200 BC, but these are not as pertinent to the social customs and covenants of the patriarchs. The first tablets from Nuzi surfaced in about 1896, but excavations at the site did not begin until 1925.

found in the patriarchal narratives of Genesis that were particular to the culture of Mesopotamia around 2000–1500 BC.

A few of the customs appear to be unique to the time period, while other tablets illuminate historical context or language. A few known tablets from Nuzi show customs of adoption of indirect heirs for childless couples similar to the process mentioned by Abram when he had followed this custom and assumed adoption of Eliezer of Damascus as his heir because he and Sarah had not been able to have their own children.

The odd instance of Esau selling his birthright to Jacob is also a practice found in the Nuzi archive, in which one tablet describes the transaction between two family members of an inheritance share of an orchard being sold for three sheep.

The act of having children by proxy is another social custom recorded in the Nuzi tablets, matching the situation of both Sarah and Rachel when they used another woman as a proxy to bear children.

The Nuzi tablets likewise contain a custom of deathbed blessing, which is found in the context of Isaac blessing Jacob and Jacob blessing his grandsons Ephraim and Manasseh, and yet is not recorded in later periods.

The type of engagement and marriage arrangements shown in the story of Jacob and Rachel were also apparently followed at Nuzi, which was geographically near where Rachel was living in northern Mesopotamia. Furthermore, marriage relations seen as culturally appropriate by the patriarchs in Genesis, such as Abraham marrying his half sister, Jacob marrying two sisters, Judah and Simeon marrying Canaanites, and Joseph marrying an Egyptian, were all later banned by the Mosaic Law in the 15th century BC, and following that time either not practiced or severely condemned.

Leah and Rachel also complained that their father "consumed our money" or dowry, which is a phrase known from Nuzi in reference to a father withholding the dowry. The drive for Rachel to steal the teraphim from her father, Laban, is also explained by the Nuzi tablets, which contain the same word and illuminate the importance of the teraphim. These teraphim were sacred objects and family heirlooms, usually in the form of a small idol, and good fortune or blessing was associated with having possession of them. According to a document from Nuzi, the teraphim would be passed down only through the son and heir of the family, and therefore it is understandable that Rachel would have to steal the teraphim because she would not have received it as an inheritance and was upset that she did not receive her dowry.

> *"I am [Yahweh] who brought you out of Ur of the Chaldeans, to give you this land to possess it... Bring Me a three year old heifer, and a three year old female goat, and a three year old ram, and a turtledove, and a young pigeon." Then [Abram] brought all these to Him and cut them in two and laid each half opposite the other (Genesis 15:7-10).*

(10) Camels and the Patriarchs
(Camel Riders Cylinder Seal)

Date: 1800 BC
Discovered: Syria
Period: Patriarchs
Keywords: camel; animal domestication; Jacob; Job
Bible Passages: Genesis 24:28-64; Job 1:1-17

Camels, both the dromedary (single hump) and the Bactrian (double hump) types, were used in the ancient Near East as pack animals, for transportation, for their milk, and even for their hair. Although debate continues as to the exact date when camels were first used as domesticated animals in the Near East, and especially when they began to be used for transportation in particular regions, archaeological evidence suggests that this had probably happened by at least 2000 BC around the beginning of the Middle Bronze Age.

For example, a cylinder seal of carved hematite and measuring 2.8 cm tall by 1.3 cm in diameter, found in Syria and dated to about 1800–1650 BC, shows two people riding on the humps of a Bactrian camel. These figures, which were probably representing a king and queen, indicate that the idea of riding camels was already known in northern Mesopotamia and the Levant[15] by this time.

Documents such as a Sumerian text from Nippur in about 1900 BC mentioning camel milk, a tablet from Ugarit dated to about 1900 BC including a camel in a list of domesticated animals, and a 15th-century BC ration list from Alalakh

---

[15] *Levant:* A region of the Middle East including modern Syria, Jordan, Lebanon, Israel, and the Palestinian territories.

recording food for a camel demonstrate that camels had been domesticated by the Middle Bronze Age.

In Egypt, petroglyphs[16] from the Old Kingdom at Aswan and from the Middle Kingdom at Wadi Nasib depict camels being used as pack animals. Far to the east, in Turkmenistan, models of Bactrian camels yoked to carts were discovered that date to about 2600 BC. Bioartifacts, such as camel bones and even woven camel hair from the 3rd millennium BC, have been discovered at excavations in Persia, Arabia, Egypt, and the Levant, suggesting that camels were kept in cities as domesticated animals.

During the Middle Bronze Age in Mesopotamia, the Levant, and Egypt at the time of Abraham, Isaac, and Laban, camels are mentioned in the book of Genesis as transportation, pack animals, and for milk, which coincides with archaeological finds concerning camels in this period.

> *Then [he] unloaded the camels, and he gave straw and feed to the camels (Genesis 24:32).*

---

[16] *Petroglyphs:* Images or writing carved into a large rock surface.

(11) MIGRATING TO EGYPT
(Tomb of Khnumhotep II)

Date: 12th Dynasty of Egypt, about 1870 BC

Discovered: Tomb of Khnumhotep II, Beni Hasan, Egypt

Period: Patriarchs

Keywords: Semites; Asiatics; immigration; shepherds; nomads; tunic

Bible Passages: Genesis 37:3-28; 46:1-7

The tomb of Khnumhotep II, who was a nomarch[17] of Oryx during the reigns of Amenemhat II and Senusret II, was decorated with elaborate wall paintings and accompanying inscriptions that recount events and lifestyle in 19th century BC Egypt. Inside his tomb at Beni Hassan, Egypt, part of the wall painting from

---

[17] *Nomarch:* The ruler or governor of a nome, or province, in ancient Egypt.

about 1870 BC depicts a group of pastoral, nomadic Semites[18] entering Egypt from Canaan with their livestock and spices during the reign of Pharaoh Senusret II.[19] Men, women, children, animals, and supplies were painted on the panel in colorful detail, giving insight into the look and style of people from Canaan in the time of the patriarchs. The leader or chieftain of this group, Abi-Shai, is shown following the Egyptian man Khety, overseer of hunters, who was their escort within Egypt. During the Middle Kingdom and Second Intermediate Period, before the Hyksos expulsion in the 16th century BC, people from western Asia were able to cross into Egypt more easily.

On the panel, a multicolored tunic, which was a fashionable and expensive piece of clothing from Canaan, is also showcased. Joseph, son of Jacob, was given a similar multicolored tunic as a gift from his father before he was sold into slavery by his jealous brothers. Eventually, the patriarch or chieftain Jacob, along with his entire family, immigrated to Egypt from Canaan in the early 17th century BC and were given a designated area to settle in Egypt, similar to what had occurred with Abi-Shai and his people decades earlier.

> *They took their livestock and their property, which they had acquired in the land of Canaan, and came to Egypt, Jacob and all his descendants with him (Genesis 46:6).*

---

[18] *Semite:* A designation referring to people of the ancient world who spoke a Semitic language, including Akkadian, Ammonite, Aramaic, Assyrian, Babylonian, Canaanite, Edomite, Hebrew, Moabite, Phoenician, and Ugaritic. The ancient Egyptians often referred to all people from western Asia as *Asiatics.*

[19] While this would be slightly earlier than when Joseph and subsequently his father, Jacob, arrive in Egypt, the events occur in the same general historical period. According to archaeological excavations and information derived from various ancient documents and artwork, during this time large numbers of people from western Asia immigrated into Egypt and settled primarily in the Nile Delta region, just as Jacob and his family also did. Following this period, the Egyptian pharaoh Ahmose I retook Lower Egypt and began enslaving Semites or Asiatics—an Egyptian designation for people from the area of greater Canaan that would have included the Hebrews and other tribal groups (Exodus 1:6-14). The transition from a pharaoh who did not know Joseph to the forced labor of the Hebrews and other Semites seems to fit the transition from the rule of the Hyksos to the 18th Dynasty and the subsequent policy of forced labor upon Asiatics and other non-Egyptians.

(12) JACOB AND JOSEPH IN EGYPT
(Jacob-El and Sheshi Scarabs)

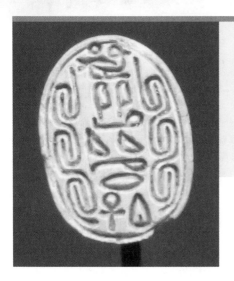

Date: 1800–1600 BC

Discovered: Egypt, Canaan, Nubia

Period: Patriarchs

Keywords: Jacob; scarab; Yaqob; Joseph

Bible Passages: Genesis 25:24-26; 41:14-49; 46:1-28

Names often illuminate historical periods and chronologies, so inscribed scarab[20] seals, primarily containing names of kings, officials, and others in positions of power, can be extremely useful. Typically, the seal would be attached to a ring, allowing the wearer to imprint the name onto clay or wax. These scarab seals were first made and used by the Egyptians, but the practice was later adopted by the Hyksos rulers and by people in Canaan.

Many scarab seals discovered in both Egypt and Canaan contain the names of rulers mentioned in the Bible, and in one case a personal name of one of the patriarchs known from the narratives in Genesis. At present, 27 scarab seals bearing the name "Yaqob" (Jacob) and the element "El" (perhaps meaning "protected by God") have been discovered in Egypt, Canaan, and Nubia dating to around 1800–1600 BC.[21]

---

[20] *Scarab:* In ancient Egypt, small amulets or seals in the shape of the scarab beetle were carved out of stone or made from faience, and often inscribed with the name of a king or official in Egyptian hieroglyphs.

[21] The date range places the original manufacture of the Yaqob scarabs in the Second Intermediate Period of Egypt and preceding the time of the Hyksos 15th Dynasty.

While the scarabs may not be referring to Jacob the patriarch and father of the 12 tribes, these inscriptions do attest to the usage of the name Yaqob/Jacob in Canaan and Egypt during the time of the Jacob known from Genesis around the 18th century BC. Further, it is significant that the name does not appear to be com-

mon either before or after that period, demonstrating that the name Jacob was primarily used at the time of the patriarchs and therefore the narratives in Genesis accurately reflect the historical usage of this name.

Another scarab type possibly connected to Joseph and his time in Egypt are those of the 14th Dynasty king or pharaoh named Sheshi, who seems to have ruled for around 40 years during the 18th and 17th centuries BC. Often referred to as Maaibre Sheshi, he is the best attested pharaoh of the second Intermediate Period with 396 currently known seals attributed to him, implying his power. The seals were found throughout Lower Egypt, Upper Egypt, Nubia, and Canaan, indicating that his kingdom or influence spread throughout Egypt and beyond instead of only being a regional ruler.

Further, there is evidence for a long famine in Egypt soon after his reign. Based on the time period of his rule, extent of his power and influence, the famine, and evidence showing that Semites served in the Egyptian government at the time, it is possible that Sheshi could have been the unnamed pharaoh under whom Joseph served for many years.

All the persons of the house of Jacob, who came to Egypt, were seventy (Genesis 46:27).

(13) THE EARLY PHILISTINES
(Phaistos Disk)

Date: 1800 BC

Discovered: Phaistos, Crete

Period: Patriarchs

Keywords: Crete; Minoan; Philistines; Caphtor

Bible Passages: Genesis 21:32-34; 26:1-18; Deuteronomy 2:23; 1 Chronicles 1:12; Jeremiah 47:4; Amos 9:7

The Phaistos Disk was discovered in an underground chamber among ashes and burnt bovine bones, in what was referred to as a "temple depository" located northeast of the main area of the Minoan palace in the ancient city of Phaistos on the southern side of the island of Crete. Nearby, Linear A tablet PH1 was also discovered. Made of baked clay, the Phaistos Disk measures approximately 6.3 inches (16 cm) in diameter and about 0.4 inches (1 cm) in thickness. It was likely created around 1800–1600 BC on Crete.

Stamped on both sides with symbols in a circular spiraling arrangement, many of the signs have parallels to those known from Linear A, while others match Linear B. Linear A is an undeciphered ancient writing system used by the Minoans from about 1800–1450 BC, while Linear B, which immediately succeeded it, was a similar looking writing system that was used to write the earliest known form of the Greek language. The text of the Phaistos Disk is probably syllabic, although it has also been suggested as ideographic, hieroglyphic,[22] or a combination. 45 unique signs appear on the disk, with a total of 242 signs divided into 61 "words" or sections impressed into the clay. Artifacts such as the Arkalochori Axe and the Mavro Spilio ring contain several similar signs and confirm the authenticity of the Phaistos Disk.

The most recent attempt at decipherment suggests that the disk is a religious text mentioning the goddess of love, Aphaia. The head wearing a plumed headdress is the most common sign on the disk, appearing 19 times, and it may connect the Sea Peoples (including the Philistines mentioned in Genesis) shown on the Medinet Habu reliefs of Rameses III with people from the island of Crete, placing this group on Crete at a period far earlier than the 12th century BC invasion of Egypt and the Levant by the Sea Peoples.

According to the books of Deuteronomy, 1 Chronicles, Jeremiah, and Amos, the Philistines came from Caphtor, which seems to have been one of the ancient designations for Crete. Excavations at Gerar, Tel Kabri, and Ashkelon on the coast of Canaan have all uncovered evidence of Minoan culture, demonstrating that early Philistines from Crete had migrated to Canaan by the Middle Bronze Age during the time of the patriarchs.

So Isaac went to Gerar, to Abimelech king of the Philistines (Genesis 26:1).

---

[22] *Hieroglyphics:* Any form of writing which uses pictures to represent letters or sounds. The most famous hieroglyphic writing system of the ancient world was used in Egypt.

(14) The Golden Necklace
(Gold of Valor)

Date: 1330 BC

Discovered: Saqqara, tomb of Horemheb

Period: Judges

Keywords: Joseph; necklace

Bible Passage: Genesis 41:25-45

The Gold of Valor or Gold of Honor was an ancient Egyptian award, usually in the form of a large gold necklace, given to those who performed exceptional service to the pharaoh and the nation. The practice goes back to before 1600 BC during the Second Intermediate Period and around the lifetime of Joseph. The Egyptian pharaohs Kamose and Ahmose I awarded the Gold of Valor necklace to Queen

Ahhotep for her support in the war against the Hyksos in the 16th century BC. The Gold of Valor was also bestowed twice on the military official Ahmose son of Ebana for his exceptional service in battles for the pharaoh.

Further, the discovery of a ceremonial offering of severed enemy hands found at Avaris, which according to Egyptian texts was an offering that could result in receiving the Gold of Valor honor, demonstrates that this Egyptian custom had been adopted by the Hyksos and was also used in northern Egypt at the time when Joseph lived and served in the royal court.[23]

High-ranking soldiers and officers of the king, such as Horemheb and Ay during the 18th Dynasty, also received this award. In the tomb of Horemheb at Saqqara, a stone relief depicts him receiving the Gold of Valor for his exceptional service as commander of the army. Ironically, Horemheb demolished many of the monuments of Akhenaten and Atenism once he became pharaoh, reverting to the old ways and reversing what had been done by the pharaohs he had served.

After Joseph interpreted for the pharaoh a dream about a future famine, then advised the king that they should gather 20 percent of their produce during the good years and store it under guard for the coming years of famine, the pharaoh awarded Joseph the "gold necklace" or Gold of Valor for wisdom that would save Egypt.[24]

Then Pharaoh took off his signet ring from his hand and put it on Joseph's hand, and clothed him in garments of fine linen and put the gold necklace around his neck (Genesis 41:42).

---

[23] Joseph was also given a new Egyptian name, Zaphenath-paneah, which is a practice attested in Papyrus Brooklyn of the 17th century BC, when servants with Semitic names were given new Egyptian names. The Egyptian rendering of the name Zaphenath-paneah and its exact meaning are debated, but "the god speaks, he lives" and "he who is called life" are two popular suggestions.

[24] It is also possible that the memory of the seven-year famine, divine dream of the pharaoh, and interpretation and solution by a wise advisor was preserved on the 3rd-century BC Famine Stele, although the inscription on the stele refers to Pharaoh Djoser, who lived centuries before Joseph.

(15) JOB AND THE CONVERSATION WITH GOD
(Dialogue Between a Man and His God)

Date: 1700 BC

Discovered: Mesopotamia

Period: Patriarchs

Keywords: wisdom; Job; dialogue; suffering; theodicy

Bible Passage: Job 38:1–42:10

An ancient poem written in Akkadian by an author named Kalbanum, tentatively dated to around 1700 BC and referred to as "A Dialogue Between a Man and His God," addresses a righteous man suffering and his conversation with a god. It is known from only one existing copy, consisting of 69 lines on the front and back of a tablet recovered from southern Mesopotamia. Wisdom literature from Mesopotamia and Egypt has been preserved from this period and seems to have been a prevalent theme at the time, although the wisdom genre from Egypt usually focused on stating wise principles rather than on human suffering.

The poem begins by describing the dire situation of the man, lamentation to his lord the god, and his question about why he is suffering since he does not know what sin or sins he has committed. The middle section is fragmentary and thus difficult to understand. Near the end of the poem the god states that he is creator, helper, protector, and provider of eternal life. It concludes with an exhortation and promise of prosperity to the man, who then makes a final prayer that the god would make his way straight and his path open. A personal god addressing a suppliant in this manner is unique in ancient Mesopotamian literature.

Due to obvious similarities, "Dialogue" has been compared thematically to the book of Job from the Bible. Both are in poetic form, both have a protagonist who undergoes unjust suffering, both have communication between god and man, and both have a resolution at the end of the story. According to a few historical markers in the text, the setting for the book of Job can be placed in the general period that this Akkadian poem was composed, or just before. The poem shows that these questions were being explored and written down around the time of Job. While the basics are similar, Job is clearly monotheistic, explains the suffering was due to Satan, and is considerably longer.[25]

> *Then Job answered [Yahweh] and said, "I know that You can do all things...I will ask You, and You instruct me."...[Yahweh] restored the fortunes of Job when he prayed for his friends, and [Yahweh] increased all that Job had twofold (Job 42:1,4,10).*

---

[25] A similar Babylonian text called Ludlul Bel Nemeqi, or "I Will Praise the Lord of Wisdom," dates to about 1000 BC. The author questions the god Marduk about why he has been forsaken and describes his suffering. Eventually, the man has a series of dreams in which Marduk sends messengers and finally relieves his suffering. The story then ends with praise and sacrifice to Marduk. This poem, though polytheistic and Babylonian in its theology, has been compared thematically to the book of Job. The basics are similar, but Job has clearly different theology, explanations, is much longer, and his life predates the composition of Ludlul Bel Nemeqi by centuries.

CHAPTER 2

The Israelites in Egypt, Exodus, and the Wilderness

(Exodus–Deuteronomy)

For most modern scholars of archaeology, ancient history, and the Bible, the events of the Exodus and wandering are considered mythological. These scholars declare that there is no evidence that Hebrews lived in Egypt, no evidence related to events of the Exodus, and no evidence of the Israelites wandering in the wilderness. Several artifacts, however, suggest otherwise and actually support many elements of the Exodus and wandering narratives.

Israelite life in Egypt and the Jews subsequent enslavement there, the Exodus led by Moses, and the wandering in the wilderness were recorded in the books of Exodus, Leviticus, Numbers, and Deuteronomy.

Previously, the family of Jacob had settled in the northeastern Nile Delta region and multiplied their population over following generations. However, when the Egyptians from the south conquered the north and established the 18th Dynasty (ca. 1570 BC), a pharaoh who had no knowledge of Joseph took over the area and enslaved the Semites originally from western Asia, including the family of Israelites who had become a numerous people.

After many years, Moses returned from his exile to Midian and requested that the pharaoh let the Israelites leave Egypt to worship God. But the pharaoh refused, and 10 plagues ravaged the land before the Israelites were able to leave. Once free from the grip of the pharaoh, however, the people wandered for about 40 years in the wilderness until finally going to the Promised Land of Canaan in the Late Bronze Age (ca. 1500–1200 BC).

According to chronological information from the Bible, these events spanned a period of almost 300 years, while geographic information places the events in Egypt until the wilderness wandering period. In this section, the majority of the artifacts are Egyptian and originate primarily from this time or are directly related to the events of the period. These artifacts include papyri, artwork, and official stone inscriptions that document or illuminate the time in which the Israelites were in Egypt, the Exodus itself, and the period of the wandering.

(16) Hebrew Servants in Egypt
(Papyrus Brooklyn)

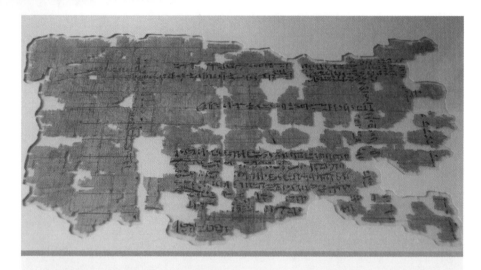

Date: 17th century BC
Discovered: Thebes (?), Egypt
Period: Exodus
Keywords: slaves; servants; Hebrews; Joseph; Shiphrah; papyrus
Bible Passages: Genesis 41:45; Exodus 1:5-22

An Egyptian list of domestic servants recorded on a papyrus[26] from about the 17th century BC contains not only Semitic names but even Hebrew names. This period came just after the life of Joseph and preceded the Exodus, which was the time that the Hebrews lived in Egypt as settlers and then as slaves.

A section of this papyrus contains a list of 95 servants, many of whom are

---

[26] *Papyrus/Papyri:* An early writing material similar to paper, made from the papyrus plant.

specified as Asiatic or coming from western Asia (primarily Canaan).[27] The servants with foreign names are given Egyptian names, just as Joseph was after he was promoted from a household servant under Potiphar to the role of vizier over all Egypt. The majority of the names are feminine because domestic servants were typically female.

Approximately 30 of the servants have names identified as Semitic, but more relevant to the Exodus story is that 9 of these servants appear to have specifically Hebrew names. The Hebrew names found on the list include: Menahema, a feminine form of Menahem (2 Kings 15:14); Ashera, a feminine form of Asher, the name of one of the sons of Jacob (Genesis 30:13); Shiphrah, the name of one of the Hebrew midwives prior to the Exodus (Exodus 1:15); 'Aqoba, a name appearing to be a feminine form of Jacob or Yaqob (Genesis 25:26); Sekera, which is either a feminine name similar to Issachar, a name of one of the sons of Jacob, or simply the feminine form of Issachar (Genesis 30:18); Dawidi-huat, a compound name utilizing the name David (1 Samuel 16:13); Esebtw, a name derived from the Hebrew word *eseb* meaning "herb" (Deuteronomy 32:2); Hayah-wr, another compound name composed of Hayah or Eve (Genesis 3:20); and finally the name Hy'b'rw, which appears to be an Egyptian transcription of "Hebrew" (Genesis 39:14).

Therefore, this list is a clear attestation of Hebrews living in Egypt prior to the Exodus under Moses, in their earlier period of residence in the country prior to their total enslavement, and perhaps shows that a group may have migrated south or was taken south for work.

Then the king of Egypt spoke to the Hebrew midwives, one of whom was named Shiphrah (Exodus 1:15).

---

[27] This Second Intermediate Period document was rediscovered on the antiquities market and designated Papyrus Brooklyn 35.1446. Several references to Thebes on the papyrus indicate that it was originally composed in or around that city, the capital of Upper Egypt. The dates for the pharaohs from this period are often tentative and highly disputed, so it is difficult to date anything with absolute certainty. However, the papyrus mentions the pharaoh called Sobekhotep, who seems to have reigned around 1700 BC.

(17) Brickmaking Slaves in Egypt
(Tomb of Rekmire)

Date: 1450 BC

Discovered: Valley of the Nobles, Egypt

Period: Exodus

Keywords: slavery; bricks; Rameses; Pithom; Heliopolis

Bible Passages: Exodus 1:11; 2:11; 5:4-19

On this tomb mural from the time of Pharaoh Thutmose III, a variety of slaves, including Asiatic or Semitic slaves, perform tasks for the Egyptians. In particular, the slaves make bricks using mud and straw formed in a mold, dried in the sun, and then transported for use in construction projects.

During the New Kingdom in Egypt, slavery of Asiatics was so common that the Egyptian word *Aamu* (Asiatic) came to be synonymous with slave. The Hebrews prior to the Exodus were part of this slave labor force and often made mud bricks for state building projects. The making of mud bricks by Hebrew slaves and the difficulties in this task are detailed in the Exodus account, and a hieroglyphic text about an Egyptian master reminding slaves to not be idle lest they receive a beating with the rod brings to mind the episode in which Moses saw an Egyptian taskmaster beating a Hebrew slave.

Another Egyptian text, called the Louvre Leather Roll, describes a situation similar to what is recorded in Exodus—that in this time period quotas of bricks were imposed on slaves, but when they did not have the necessary materials to complete all of the bricks, such as a lack of straw, the slaves were punished.

The transition from a pharaoh who did not know Joseph to the forced labor of the Hebrews and other Semites seems to fit the transition from the rule of the Hyksos to the 18th Dynasty and the subsequent policy of forced labor upon Asiatics and other non-Egyptians.

Papyri such as Leningrad Papyrus 1116A from the 18th Dynasty, probably the reign of Pharaoh Thutmose III prior to around 1450 BC, specifies that immigrant people were subjected to compulsory labor such as public building projects after the expulsion of the Hyksos under Pharaoh Ahmose I and subsequent rulers. This would be exactly the time of the enslavement of the Hebrews.

Just as Egyptian documents and this wall painting demonstrate that Asiatics or Semites were forced to construct public buildings, the book of Exodus records that the Hebrews were involved in constructing storage buildings in the cities of Rameses, Pithom, and On (Heliopolis).

> *You are no longer to give the people straw to make brick as previously; let them go and gather straw for themselves. But the quota of bricks which they were making previously, you shall impose on them (Exodus 5:7-8).*

(18) PHARAOH AND THE HARDENING HEART
(The Negative Confession)

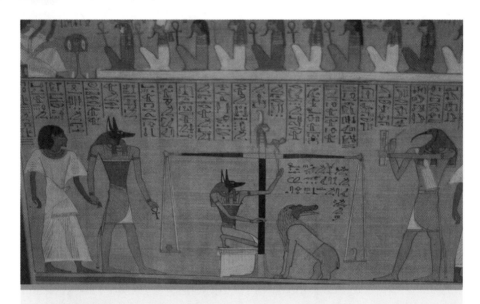

Date: 1300 BC

Discovered: Memphis (?), Egypt

Period: Exodus

Keywords: afterlife; underworld; heart

Bible Passage: Exodus 7:13–9:35

The Weighing of the Heart ceremony in ancient Egypt was a procedure that the Egyptians believed occurred after death in the underworld, and it would judge if an individual was allowed to pass on to paradise or "the fields of Aaru" based upon their deeds in life. Associated spells were found in the Book of the Dead, and it was connected to the 42 Negative Confessions, which seems to have originated around 1570 BC at the beginning of the 18th Dynasty—the period in which Moses was born.

Depicted on papyri and the walls of tombs, the Weighing of the Heart typically showed the deceased in front of scales with their heart weighed against the feather of Ma'at (truth, order, justice), in the presence of the god Anubis, the demon Ammit, and the god Osiris.

One of the most famous of these depictions is found in the Book of the Dead chapter 125 prepared for Hunefer, an Egyptian scribe who lived around 1300 BC. The book was illustrated in full color with accompanying hieroglyphic text on a long roll of papyrus.[28]

During the process of confessions, the individual would recite a list of 42 sins that they did not commit, and although the number remained consistent, the list of sins varied from person to person. The focus was on intent rather than result, which means it was easier to access paradise than a standardized list of sins committed. One spell even invoked the heart to not weigh down the balance nor testify against the deceased, and if effective this would allow the individual to pass the test even if certain sins had been done.

On the scales, overseen by Anubis, the heart would be weighed against the feather, since the Egyptians believed that the heart was made "heavy" with sin. This is why the heart was left in mummified bodies, while other organs were removed. If judged pure, indicating a virtuous life, the heart would not outweigh the feather and that person could proceed to Osiris and go on to paradise. However, if the heart was heavy and weighed more than the feather of truth, the individual was judged to be evil and unworthy. The consequence for failing the test was that their heart would be consumed by Ammit, a strange demon goddess shown as a creature who was part lion, crocodile, and hippopotamus.[29]

Ancient texts vary about the status of the deceased after their heart was devoured, but either their soul would be restless forever or the person would cease to exist.

The Egyptian theological concept of the heart being made heavy by evil deeds or sin is alluded to in the Exodus story, when Moses wrote that the pharaoh "made his heart heavy" when he rejected the messages and warnings from God spoken through Moses and continued to disbelieve God even through the punishments of the plagues.

> *Pharaoh hardened his heart [lit. "made his heart heavy"] this time also, and he did not let the people go (Exodus 8:32).*

---

[28] The section of the papyrus showing the weighing of the heart process measures about 34.4 inches long (87.5 cm) and 15.7 inches tall (40 cm). The paint colors have all been exceptionally preserved except for fading of the yellow.

[29] The Papyrus of Ani also has a famous depiction of the weighing of the heart from the same general time period, although many pieces of artwork or texts describing the ritual have been discovered in Egypt.

(19) THE POETIC PLAGUES
(Admonitions of an Egyptian Sage)

Date: 13th century BC

Discovered: Saqqara (?), Egypt

Period: Exodus

Keywords: plagues; Ipuwer; chaos

Bible Passage: Exodus 7:14–12:36

An ancient Egyptian text, written by a man named Ipuwer and referred to as the Admonitions of an Egyptian Sage, was a poetic lamentation addressed to the "All Lord," who is typically understood to be the sun god Ra. The poem describes a time in which the natural order in Egypt was severely disrupted by death, destruction, and plagues.

The only surviving copy of the papyrus dates to the 13th century BC—perhaps as early as 1300 BC. While most scholars suggest it was originally written in the Second Intermediate Period due to content, the linguistics of the text and the date of the copy indicate that it was composed during the 18th Dynasty around the 16th–14th centuries BC.

The name Ipuwer is also know from inscriptions of the 18th Dynasty, and in particular one from the time of Hatshepsut and Thutmose III just prior to the Exodus. Any historical events mentioned in the text must have occurred prior to the 13th century BC and possibly in the 18th Dynasty. If the Admonitions describes events similar to the plagues recorded in Exodus, and the Egyptian account was composed in the same general time period as the events of the Exodus, then it is plausible that the two documents contain independent accounts of the identical episode in history but from different perspectives.

Passages in the poem, such as the river being blood, blood everywhere, plague and pestilence throughout the land, the grain being destroyed, disease causing physical disfigurement, the prevalence of death, mourning throughout the land, rebellion against Ra the sun god, the death of children, the authority of the pharaoh being lost, the gods of Egypt being ineffective and losing a battle, and jewelry now being in the possession of the slaves, are all occurrences in common with the Exodus story.

Thematic and even linguistic links between the Admonitions and the plagues of Exodus have been recognized by scholars, but typically these connections are discounted on the presupposition that neither the book of Exodus nor the Admonitions of Ipuwer describe historical events, and that even if they did, the two texts would be too far separated in time from one another.

However, since the chronology may overlap, and the match in specificity of many of the events suggests the possibility that the documents are describing the same general events and period of hardship in Egypt, the Admonitions could be an Egyptian remembrance and near contemporary account of the time of the Exodus plagues.

> *"I will strike the water that is in the Nile with the staff that is in my hand, and it will be turned to blood."…And the blood was through all the land of Egypt (Exodus 7:17,21).*

(20) Pharaoh of the Exodus
(Elephantine Stele of Amenhotep II)

Date: 1440 BC

Discovered: Elephantine, Egypt

Period: Exodus

Keywords: Pharaoh; Amenhotep II; slavery; Exodus

Bible Passages: Exodus 2:11–5:1; 12:37-41; 14:4-30; Acts 7:20-30

Pharaoh Amenhotep II reigned over Egypt beginning in about 1450 BC during the powerful 18th Dynasty of the New Kingdom. His monuments and inscriptions indicate that he was one of the most boastful pharaohs of ancient Egypt, claiming such feats as being able to shoot arrows through a copper target a palm thick, rowing a ship by himself faster and farther than 200 Egyptian sailors, singlehandedly killing 7 prince warriors of Kadesh, having the kings of Babylon, the Hittites, and Mitanni all come to pay tribute to him, and supposedly conducting the largest slave raid in Egyptian history.

According to a match of chronological information from Egyptian king lists and the Bible, Amenhotep II was probably also the pharaoh of the Exodus, which occurred in approximately 1446 BC. One of the most significant artifacts relating to the circumstantial evidence for Amenhotep II being the pharaoh of the Exodus is a stele that he commissioned to commemorate one of his campaigns.

While earlier in the 18th Dynasty the Egyptians had a powerful military, especially during the reign of Thutmose III, who conducted 17 known military campaigns, after the beginning of the reign of Amenhotep II there is a steep decline. In fact, Amenhotep II had only two confirmed campaigns during his reign— the first took place prior to the Exodus, while the second was primarily a slave raid that occurred soon after the Exodus and was recorded on the Elephantine Stele.[30]

This monumental stone inscription with its accompanying artwork was originally erected at the southern city of Elephantine, and it records the campaign of Amenhotep II to Canaan in which he claims to have brought back over 101,128 captives to be used as slaves.[31] In comparison, other Egyptian military campaigns of the period brought back nowhere near the amount of captives, with the largest total being only 5,903, and as a result most scholars consider the number of slaves captured by Amenhotep II in this text to be a massive exaggeration. Because this happened right after the Exodus, perhaps it is indicative of an urgent need to replace the lost slave population in Egypt, or purely as propaganda making it appear that the pharaoh had recovered or replenished the slaves lost during the Hebrew Exodus.

> *Pharaoh and his servants had a change of heart toward the people…So he made his chariot ready and took his people with him…and he chased after the sons of Israel (Exodus 14:5-8).*

---

[30] Additional indicators include that the pharaoh preceding the Exodus must have had a reign of over 40 years, since Moses killed an Egyptian and fled to Midian for 40 years until the pharaoh who knew him had died. Thutmose III, the father and predecessor of Amenhotep II, reigned for 54 years and is the only pharaoh in the dynasty with a reign of 40 or more years. The Exodus pharaoh must also have recently begun his reign, since Moses returned and confronted the Exodus pharaoh soon after the previous pharaoh died, and Amenhotep II took the throne only about four years or less prior to the Exodus.

[31] The first campaign of Amenhotep II was launched in his third year, or approximately 1448 BC. The second campaign, to Canaan, occurred in his seventh year, approximately 1444 BC, which seems to have been only one or two years after the Exodus.

(21) THE SPHINX AND THE
DEATH OF THE FIRSTBORN
(Dream Stele)

Date: 1424 BC

Discovered: Giza, Egypt

Period: Exodus

Keywords: plagues; pharaoh; Thutmose IV; sphinx; firstborn

Bible Passage: Exodus 12:29

The Sphinx Dream Stele was found set between the paws of the Great Sphinx at Giza when the sands were uncovered and the whole monument was revealed.[32] When the Egyptian hieroglyphs were translated, it was found to be a personal yet official text of Pharaoh Thutmose IV, who reigned in the 15th century BC and was the son of Pharaoh Amenhotep II.

An illustrative scene appears at the top of the stele, showing Thutmose IV making an offering to the Great Sphinx. Below, the stone inscription claims that while Thutmose IV was out hunting one day, he rested near the Great Sphinx, fell asleep, and had a dream in which the god of the Sphinx delivered a divine message to him. Allegedly, Thutmose IV was told that if he cleared the sand from around the Sphinx, the kingship would be given to him.

The inscription indicates that Thutmose IV did not have a natural claim to the throne, forcing him to fabricate a divine promise in order to solidify his legitimacy

---

[32] The stele was carved from granite and is approximately 11.8 feet tall (3.6 m), 7.2 feet wide (2.2 m), and 2.3 feet thick (70 cm).

as the next pharaoh. Scholars consider this text to demonstrate that Thutmose IV was not the natural heir to the throne, but the death of his older brother, the firstborn and original heir, allowed him to eventually become pharaoh.

In fact, Thutmose IV had an older brother named Amenhotep who was the heir, but he mysteriously disappeared or died.[33] If Amenhotep II was the pharaoh of the Exodus, then his firstborn son and heir Amenhotep would have died during the final plague, meaning that the next son in line would eventually take the throne. This younger brother was Thutmose IV, who appears to have used "divine" propaganda to claim that the gods would grant the kingship to him as successor

to his father Amenhotep II. Because he was not the original heir, this divine invocation would make his kingship appear more legitimate to the Egyptians.

> *[Yahweh] struck all the firstborn in the land of Egypt, from the firstborn of Pharaoh who sat on his throne to the firstborn of the captive who was in the dungeon (Exodus 12:29).*

---

[33] The son and heir, Amenhotep, was a priest of Ptah according to an administrative papyrus, but he is thought to have died young, although the details of his disappearance are not known from Egyptian documents.

(22) Wandering in the Wilderness with Yahweh
(Nomads of YHWH)

Date: 1400 BC

Discovered: Soleb, Sudan

Period: Exodus

Keywords: nomads; wandering; Yahweh; Amenhotep III

Bible Passages: Exodus 7:4-7; Numbers 32:13

Hieroglyphic inscriptions mentioning the "land of the nomads of YHWH" were discovered on the walls of two New Kingdom Egyptian temples and a temple pillar in Sudan. Currently, these are the earliest known texts that contain the name YHWH (Yahweh), the name of God in the Hebrew Bible.

The first of these to be discovered, found on a topographical list at the Amara West temple, dates no earlier than ca. 1300 BC during the reign of Seti I in the 19th Dynasty, and is probably a copy of the inscription on the wall of the Soleb temple from ca. 1400 BC in the 18th Dynasty.

The Temple of Amun at Soleb was built on the left bank of the Nile, north of the Third Cataract, around 1400 BC by the 18th Dynasty pharaoh, Amenhotep III. This temple was dedicated to Amun and to Amenhotep III as a deity. When first noted by explorers, the magnificent hypostyle hall was in ruins, toppled, and partly covered by sand, but many inscriptions that had been carved into the pillars and walls had survived the millennia. Among these inscriptions was an extensive list of conquered or subdued places and people, several of whom were described as nomads.

Eighteenth Dynasty Egyptian texts repeatedly mention nomadic people living in the wilderness east of Egypt and in Canaan during the Late Bronze Age, even specifying that some were tent dwellers. The Soleb inscriptions further identify these different areas and people by associating them with a location or a deity, and at least two of the inscriptions claim defeat or subjugation of a nomadic group that worshipped Yahweh, specifically noting the "land of the nomads of YHWH" located somewhere in the Edom, Moab, and Canaan area.

Yet, the only known military campaign of Amenhotep III was to suppress a rebellion in Kush, so the claims of conquest were probably propaganda and reflect Egyptian influence from the time of Thutmose III.

One of the inscriptions was on an interior wall of the temple, following an Egyptian practice of showcasing a list naming conquered places and people. The relief on a pillar is the best preserved and shows a fragmentary bound "shasu" (nomad) prisoner with the name "land of the nomads of Yahweh" in the cartouche. Spelled phonetically, using hieroglyphs to represent the sounds Y-H-HW-W-A/E, not only do the letters match an Egyptian transliteration, but there is no "land" or "city" determinative, indicating that it must be a personal name rather than a place.

Since the only ancient people known to have worshipped Yahweh were the Israelites or Hebrews, it logically follows that these nomads were the Israelites before they settled in Canaan. This inscription is the earliest yet discovered reference to Yahweh, the personal name of God in the Hebrew Bible.

In the 15th and 14th centuries BC, the people of Yahweh, the Israelites, wandered in the wilderness like nomads and continued to live a nomadic lifestyle for many years while conquering and settling Canaan. That the name Yahweh and the nomads of Yahweh, descriptive of the Israelites, would be found on an Egyptian temple from around 1400 BC demonstrates that the Egyptians of the 18th Dynasty and the pharaoh himself were familiar with the Israelites and the God they worshipped, suggesting contact and dialogue around the time of Moses, the Exodus, and the wandering in the 15th century BC.

[Yahweh's] anger burned against Israel, and He made them wander in the wilderness forty years (Numbers 32:13).

(23) THE ARK OF THE COVENANT AND ANUBIS
(Shrine of Anubis)

Date: 14th century BC

Discovered: Valley of the Kings, KV62, Egypt

Period: Wandering

Keywords: ark of the covenant; tabernacle; shrine; Tutankhamum

Bible Passages: Exodus 25:10-22; Numbers 4:5-6; Hebrews 9:4

The Anubis Shrine or Ark of Anubis was discovered in the tomb of Tutankhamun KV62 in the Valley of the Kings and designated Shrine 261. Facing west, the direction of the Egyptian afterlife, and in front of the canopic chest of the pharaoh and the entrance to the treasury, the Anubis Shrine seems to have been set up as a guardian, and when discovered it was partially covered by a linen shirt. Although a statue of an Egyptian god was attached to the roof of the chest and the object was religious in nature, it is unlikely that it was ever used in worship, but restricted to afterlife rituals and the tomb.

The shrine measures 37 inches (95 cm) long, 15 inches (37 cm) wide, and 21.4 inches (54.3 cm) high in the shape of a trapezoid. It was constructed as a wood chest with a layer of plaster covered in gold leaf, topped with a guardian figure of

Anubis in the likeness of a jackal. Two poles were attached to the sides to carry it, and items were placed inside.[34]

The chest was decorated with the "djed pillar" associated with the afterlife and the underworld god Osiris, and two hieroglyphic inscriptions invoking Anubis. Inside the chest are four small compartments and one large compartment that contained amulets, statuettes of the god Thoth, a statuette of the god Horus, two shabtis, a clay scepter, and jewels.

This Egyptian chest comes from the 14th century BC, approximately 100 years after the Exodus and the construction of the ark of the covenant, demonstrating a crafting style used in Egypt that was also employed in the creation of the ark of the covenant. The sacred chest with a guardian on top is seen in Egyptian artwork from at least as early as the reign of Hatshepsut around 1500 BC, and therefore was an object in use in Egypt prior to the time of the Exodus.

The ark of the covenant was a chest made of acacia wood and plated in gold, measuring 2.5 cubits long, 1.5 cubits wide, and 1.5 cubits tall (approximately 52 inches long, 31 inches wide, and 31 inches tall or 1.31 m by 79 cm by 79 cm). Topped with a golden lid that had two guardian cherubim figures on it, the chest held the significant items of the two stone tablets of the Ten Commandments, the rod of Aaron, and a pot of manna. Similar to the Shrine of Anubis, it was a gold-plated wooden chest holding important items and carried by two poles, which attached to the chest, and was covered in a veil when transported.

The two chests were similar in form and construction, and demonstrate that the Israelites were familiar with Egyptian material culture of the 18th Dynasty, but beyond a general identification with religion, their function and purpose were completely different. Rather than copy the Shrine of Anubis or similar objects, the Israelite craftsmen were able to use and adapt the skills and techniques they learned in Egypt to build a sacred chest that had features unique to the worship of Yahweh and its use in the tabernacle.

> *Construct an ark of acacia wood two and a half cubits long, and one and a half cubits wide, and one and a half cubits high... overlay it with pure gold... put the poles into the rings on the sides of the ark... Make one cherub at one end and one cherub at the other end (Exodus 25:10-19).*

---

[34] With the Anubis statue attached, the total height is 46.5 inches (118 cm). The statue of Anubis was carved from wood, which was then painted black, while the collar and accents around the eyes and ears were covered with gold leaf. The eyes were made from calcite and obsidian, and the claws of silver. The shrine is currently on display at the Egyptian Museum in Cairo.

(24) BALAAM THE SEER
(Deir Alla Inscription)

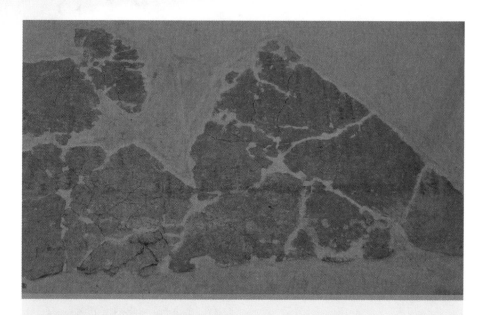

Date: 9th century BC

Discovered: Succoth (Deir Alla, Jordan)

Period: Wandering

Keywords: Balaam; curse; seer; prophecy; Balak; Aramaic

Bible Passages: Numbers 22:5–24:25; 31:8,16; Deuteronomy 23:3-5

An Aramaic text referred to as the Balaam Inscription was discovered during excavations at Deir Alla, Jordan, which is probably the site of ancient Succoth near the Jordan River. Using plaster as the medium, the poetic text had been written on a wall with black and red ink in the 9th century BC, although it told a story from centuries earlier. So far, 119 fragments have been recovered and pieced together, and although the text is still incomplete, it is significant because of its historical and religious information and its status as one of the oldest existing pieces of Aramaic literature.

The story relates how a man named Balaam, son of Beor, described as a seer or prophet, received a divine message at night from the gods, and specifically from the god El, that darkness and chaos would be coming to the land due to the work of hostile divinities. In this narrative, Balaam went through various religious rituals in an attempt to appease the gods. This section is followed by mention of the underworld. Then, the people apparently rejected, condemned, and banned Balaam and his message, but the text is unclear because of its fragmentary condition.

However, the careful and artistic composition of this text on the wall of a building indicates the importance of the story and Balaam the seer. During the Israelite wandering period, Balaam, the son of Beor from Pethor in Mesopotamia, was noted as a famous seer or prophet of great reputation and was paid by King Balak of Moab to curse the Israelites, although Balaam eventually announced oracles of blessings from Yahweh upon the Israelites instead of curses.

The existence of the Balaam Inscription demonstrates that in ancient times Balaam, son of Beor, was known as a famous seer in the area on the east side of the Jordan River where the events recorded in the book of Numbers took place.

> *So he sent messengers to Balaam son of Beor... So the elders of Moab and the elders of Midian departed with the fees for divination in their hand; and they came to Balaam (Numbers 22:5,7).*

CHAPTER 3

CONQUEST, SETTLEMENT, AND THE JUDGES
(Joshua–Ruth)

The majority of scholarly views of the conquest and settlement of Canaan by the Israelites are that it never happened or that roughly similar events happened but at a time and in a manner different from the specifics documented in the Bible. Therefore, most in academia regard the Israelite conquest and settlement to be legendary or even mythological accounts rather than history.

But what do excavations and the artifacts demonstrate regarding the periods of Joshua and the judges? Instead of being legendary, fictitious stories, archaeology demonstrates that a conquest of cities in Canaan by an outside group did occur at the places and times recorded in the books of Joshua and Judges.

The conquest and subsequent settlement of Canaan, the Promised Land, involved an initial short military campaign and distribution of the tribal territories recorded in the book of Joshua. Under the leadership of Joshua, the Israelites conducted a 5-year campaign that resulted in the burning of the cities of Jericho, Ai, and Hazor and the eradication of 31 local kings. However, there were still cities and regions in the land that the Israelites did not take possession of during the Joshua campaign, and new settlements needed to be established.

This conquest was followed by a much slower process of acquiring and settling the remaining areas in the time of the judges, documented in the books of Judges, Ruth, and the beginning of 1 Samuel, which seems to have encompassed over 300 years. All of these events occurred in Canaan, which then became the land of Israel as the new nation was established and transitioned from nomadic to sedentary life.

In this section, the artifacts presented were discovered in, originated in, or directly relate to ancient Canaan and Israel from the time in which these narratives were set—the Late Bronze Age (ca. 1500–1200 BC) and the beginning of the Iron Age (ca. 1200–1000 BC). These artifacts include royal seals, Egyptian and Canaanite documents, religious objects and artwork, and an Israelite ostracon.

(25) Jericho and Pharaoh Amenhotep III
(Scarab of Amenhotep III)

Date: 1410 BC

Discovered: Jericho, Canaan (Tell es-Sultan)

Period: Conquest

Keywords: Amenhotep III; scarab; conquest; Joshua; Hatshepsut; Thutmose III

Bible Passage: Joshua 6:20-26

Archaeological excavations at Jericho recovered a near continuous series of Egyptian royal scarabs spanning the 18th century BC to the beginning of the 14th century BC, or from the Egyptian 13th Dynasty to the middle of the 18th Dynasty. Found in tombs, these discoveries include a rare scarab of the female Pharaoh Hatshepsut, one scarab and one seal of her coregent and successor Thutmose III, and two scarabs of Amenhotep III.

The royal scarab of Hatshepsut is an artifact limited to production and use during her reign because of her unpopularity following her death, and the rare two-sided seal of Thutmose III is also probably restricted to the years of his rule due to its unique nature. The two scarabs of Amenhotep III, however, are also extremely important because those represent the latest pharaoh attested by artifacts from the Bronze Age city of Jericho and, as such, place the fall of Jericho during his reign.

Along with a 15th century BC cuneiform tablet and distinctive pottery found during excavations, including special painted wares, these scarabs suggest that the walled city of Jericho was inhabited from before 1700 BC to around 1400 BC. Then the destruction and abandonment of the city occurred during the time of Pharaoh Amenhotep III, whose reign bridged the 15th and 14th centuries BC.

One of the two Amenhotep III scarabs is of particular interest. The inscribed, flat side of the scarab contains the cartouche of the pharaoh with his throne name Neb Maat Ra (meaning "the god Ra is lord of truth/justice/order") and shows extremely fine Egyptian craftsmanship, indicating that it was manufactured in Egypt and imported to Canaan. To the left of the cartouche appears an early form of the Aten sun disk with its outstretched rays, perhaps linking it to the time when the prominence of Aten was emerging in Egypt, and when Amenhotep III was often referred to as "the Sun" in the Amarna Letters. This suggests that the scarab was made before subsequent religious reforms of extreme Atenism or the even later reversion to Amun worship.

Therefore, this Amenhotep III scarab found at Jericho would have been contemporary with his reign, indicating that the destruction and abandonment of Jericho occurred around 1400 BC, which is also the approximate date that can be ascertained from a chronological analysis of the books of Numbers, Joshua, Judges, and Kings.

[The Israelites] burned the city [of Jericho] with fire, and all that was in it. Only the silver and gold, and articles of bronze and iron, they put into the treasury of the house of [Yahweh] (Joshua 6:24).

(26) THE CURIOUS CASE OF SHECHEM
(Amarna Letters of Labayu)

Date: 1400 BC

Discovered: Akhetaten, Egypt (Tell Amarna)

Period: Conquest

Keywords: Amenhotep III; letter; Labayu; Shechem; conquest

Bible Passages: Joshua 8:33-35; 24:1-28

Of the 382 known Amarna Letters, over 150 were written from Canaanite kings to the Egyptian pharaoh Amenhotep III around 1400 BC. Among these, three were written by Labayu, king of Shechem, while in several other letters various Canaanite kings accuse Labayu of attacking them, allying with the Habiru[35] (or Hapiru), and even giving the land of the Shechem city-state to the Habiru.

In particular EA289 from Abdi-Heba of Jerusalem asked, "Are we to act like Labayu when he was giving the land of Shechem to the Habiru?" And in EA287, the sons of Labayu were similarly accused of giving land to the Habiru. However, Labayu defended himself and his actions in EA252, and in subsequent letters denied association with the Habiru or involvement in giving away the land of Shechem. Most likely, Labayu was playing a clever political game of deception,

---

[35] The designation *Habiru, Hapiru,* or *'Abiru* first appears in the 18th century BC, and then disappears from the record in the 11th century BC. Throughout the Amarna Letters, the term *Hapiru* appears frequently in reference to enemies of the Canaanite city-states who are continually raiding and conquering parts of Canaan. It is generally understood that *Habiru* or *Hapiru* was a socioeconomic term referring to a group of people who were outsiders, outcasts, fugitives, or refugees living outside of mainstream society, and nomadic or seminomadic bands led by a prominent leader. Although not an ethnic term, and therefore not exclusively equivalent with Hebrew, the understanding of the term *Habiru* does appear to fit the status of the Hebrews in the narratives about the Israelite conquest.

working with the Habiru against other Canaanite city-states while staying in favor with the pharaoh.

Although during the initial phase of the Israelite conquest when Joshua led a campaign against many cities in Canaan, Shechem stands out because no mention is made in the book of Joshua about an attack on the city. Yet all of the Israelites, along with the local residents, were recorded as gathering between Mount Gerizim and Mount Ebal at Shechem in a peaceful manner after Jericho and Ai have been destroyed, but before the treaty with Gibeon and the attack on Hazor. This assembly is repeated later in the Joshua narrative, immediately following the end of the initial campaign against the Canaanite city-states.[36]

Archaeological excavations at Shechem have also demonstrated that there was no destruction of the city until nearly 100 years after the time of Labayu and Joshua. The Amarna Letters record that Shechem was given to the Habiru, who may be linked to the Israelites by descriptions in other letters of the Habiru attacking and conquering various cities and areas in Canaan. In light of the Amarna Letters and excavations, Shechem was not conquered, but instead there may have been a peaceful agreement allowing the area of Shechem to be given to the Israelites rather than taken by force.

> *All Israel with their elders and officers and their judges were standing on both sides of the ark before the Levitical priests who carried the ark of the covenant of [Yahweh], the stranger as well as the native. Half of them stood in front of Mount Gerizim and half of them in front of Mount Ebal (Joshua 8:33).*

---

[36] The remains of a monumental standing stone found in front of the fortress temple at Shechem and probably dating to the Late Bronze Age has been suggested as the memorial stone that Joshua erected when the people made a covenant to follow God at Shechem. While this is possible, the exact date of the standing stone is unknown and therefore the identification is speculative.

(27) Child Sacrifice in Canaan
(Pozo Moro Relief)

Date: 6th century BC

Discovered: Necropolis of Pozo Moro (near Albacete, Spain)

Period: Conquest

Keywords: sacrifice; Canaanite; Phoenician; tophet

Bible Passages: Leviticus 18:21; Deuteronomy 12:31; 18:10; 2 Kings 3:26-27; 23:10; Jeremiah 32:35

The Pozo Moro monument was discovered in an ancient Phoenician graveyard in what is now southern Spain, and it shows strong influence from Phoenician and generally ancient Near Eastern iconography. Dating to the end of the 6th century BC, the scenes probably depict practices of Phoenicians who had migrated west from Canaan in the Iron Age.

The stone monument contains a variety of scenes, including one depicting child sacrifice. This particular carving shows a seated god on the left who is holding and about to consume a child inside of a bowl, a figure to the right that is offering a bowl toward the god, and a third figure with a sickle sword who is grasping another bowl with a child inside of it.

Several specialized cemeteries used to bury the burned bones of infants, fetuses, and children have been discovered in various Phoenician cemeteries around the Mediterranean, including Carthage where approximately 6,000 urns containing burned human bones were found. While child sacrifice had been adopted in Judah in the 8th and 7th centuries BC until King Josiah destroyed the *tophets* (locations or fiery ovens associated with human sacrifice by fire) and put an end to the rituals, human sacrifice had been practiced centuries earlier in Canaan.

At the Amman Airport Temple from around 1400 BC, a large outdoor square stone altar was discovered with over 1,000 burned bone fragments, the majority of which were human remains. This human sacrifice was probably associated with the cult of Milkom (Molech), which is attested by a dedicatory inscription and temple at the Amman citadel only about 4 km from the Airport Temple.

A 13th-century BC text from Ugarit, north of Canaan, also mentions the offering of a child to Ba'al in order to drive away an attacking enemy from the city, which is a practice shown on a 13th-century BC stone relief in Egypt depicting the siege of Ashkelon by the Egyptians.

The offering of humans through fire sacrifice to a deity as mentioned in the Bible is found in ancient artwork, multiple texts from antiquity, and a few archaeological sites.

> *For every abominable act which [Yahweh] hates they have done for their gods; for they even burn their sons and daughters in the fire to their gods (Deuteronomy 12:31).*

(28) ISRAEL IN CANAAN
(The Merneptah Stele)

Date: 19th Dynasty, reign of Merneptah, ca. 1219 BC

Discovered: Temple of Merneptah, Thebes

Period: Conquest and Judges

Keywords: Merneptah; Israel; Ashkelon; Gezer; Yanoam; judges; pharaoh

Bible Passage: Judges 1:1-33

The question of when the Israelites arrived and settled in Canaan, and the evidence for their appearance, is an important debate that revolves around several archaeological sites and a few key artifacts. The most important of these artifacts is the Merneptah Stele, an Egyptian stone monument about 10.4 feet (3.18 meters) tall with a 28-line hieroglyphic inscription describing campaigns of Pharaoh Merneptah against Libya and Canaan in the late 13th century BC.[37]

On the top of the stele, Merneptah is seen with the Egyptian gods Amun, Mut, and Khonsu. In the section about Canaan, taking place in year five of his reign around 1219 BC, the text mentions that the region of Canaan was plundered,

---

[37] Pharaoh Merneptah was the king of Egypt from about 1224–1214 BC, and like many other pharaohs, he led military campaigns that he had documented in official Egyptian records. Originally a stele of Amenhotep III, Merneptah inscribed the blank side of the stele for his feats, then had it erected at his funerary temple in Thebes. Joshua probably died around 1370 BC, at which point the Israelites still had to defeat Canaanites and begin to settle more of the land, eventually becoming the most populous and dominant group, but this took time, as the book of Judges records. Merneptah arrived in Canaan about 150 years later, about the time of Deborah and Barak, when the Israelites had cities and towns throughout the land.

the cities of Ashkelon, Gezer, and Yanoam were conquered, and that the seed or grain of the people Israel was destroyed. A portion of the text translates as: "Canaan has been plundered into every sort of woe. Ashkelon has been overcome. Gezer has been captured. Yano'am is made nonexistent. Israel is laid waste and its seed (grain) is not."

This 13th-century BC official Egyptian text, commemorating victories of the pharaoh, is the earliest widely acknowledged inscription mentioning the name Israel. Although alternative explanations have been suggested, the hieroglyphs and the context clearly demonstrate that it refers to the people Israel of the Bible, which is the only known Israel in ancient history.

The record on the stele was fashioned to begin with a region, noting three cities that were situated in the south, central, and north, and to end with a people that inhabited the land. The Israel section of the inscription spells out the name Israel with Egyptian hieroglyphs, then is followed by a symbol signifying that the word refers to a group of people, not a location.

The reference to Israel as the only people mentioned in the region demonstrates that the Israelites were the dominant group in Canaan in the late 13th century BC, and it indicates that they had been present in the region for a significant amount of time prior to the campaign of Merneptah. If the Israelites began to settle Canaan after 1400 BC as the books of Joshua and Judges describe, then by the time of Merneptah they would have been the main occupants of the land rather than the Canaanites, just as the stele indicates.

> *It came about when Israel became strong, that they put the Canaanites to forced labor, but they did not drive them out completely. Ephraim did not drive out the Canaanites who were living in Gezer, so the Canaanites lived in Gezer among them (Judges 1:28-29).*

(29) Ashtarte and the Asherah
(Astarte Plaque)

Date: 13th century BC

Discovered: Lachish, Israel

Period: Judges

Keywords: Astarte; Asherah; goddess; idol

Bible Passages: Deuteronomy 16:21-22; Judges 2:13; 6:25-30; 10:6; 1 Kings 11:5; 18:19

Astarte or Ashtarte was one of the primary goddesses in the ancient Near East, worshipped throughout the region of Canaan especially in the Bronze and Iron Ages, and attested archaeologically in cuneiform tablets, inscriptions, plaques, and stelae. Astarte has even been found in Egyptian documents and artwork as early as the 16th century BC, due to migrants from Canaan bringing their religious beliefs into Egypt during the Second Intermediate Period.

The prominence and specific roles of Astarte varied according to the region or period, but in general she was regarded as a fertility and war deity, similar to the Mesopotamian goddess Ishtar with whom she was linguistically and functionally connected. Often the symbols and characteristics of Astarte also overlapped with Anat the war goddess, but in certain systems the two were clearly distinct goddesses.

Ancient depictions of Astarte usually render her in the nude, and frequently with a lion or horse and an astral symbol. In Phoenicia, such as at Sidon, Tyre, Byblos, and Beirut, she was particularly prominent, and King Solomon adopted this goddess through his connections with Phoenicia.

Astarte was also widely worshipped by the earlier Canaanites as a fertility goddess and consort of Ba'al, demonstrated by discoveries of ceramic and metallic representations from Canaan dating to the Middle and Late Bronze Ages, including a gold plaque of the 13th century BC found at Lachish, which measures 20.4 cm tall and 11.2 cm wide.

During the time of the judges, many Israelites were influenced by Canaanite beliefs, rejecting strict monotheism and adopting deities such as Astarte (Ashtoreth) into their personal religious systems so that they worshipped Yahweh alongside pagan gods and goddesses.

However, Astarte the goddess was distinct from the Asherah mentioned in the Bible, which was a sacred tree or pole representing a deity. The word or name *Asherah* appears in the books of Deuteronomy, Judges, Kings, and Chronicles. Some scholars have equated certain texts, inscriptions, statuettes, and drawings with the Asherah, identified the Asherah of the Bible as a goddess, and claimed that a goddess named Asherah was the consort of Yahweh.

Instead, the usage of *Asherah* in the Hebrew Bible indicates not a goddess but a wooden religious object—a sacred tree or pole—that was associated with religious worship of a prominent deity. In addition to being identified in the Bible as a tree or wooden object, the Asherah is never referred to as a deity, a statue, an anthropomorphic representation, or a sentient being.

Another image of a goddess, probably Ashtarte, carved from limestone in the form of a standing idol 20.8 cm tall, was found in Nahariya and dates to around the 19th to 17th centuries BC. This pole-form type of idol may have been an influence on the Asherah pole made by the Israelites, but an important distinction existed in that the Ashtarte idol was an image with a face and body, while the Asherah was merely a blank pole or tree.

Further, a goddess named Asherah is not mentioned in any known Phoenician inscriptions of the 1st millennium BC, and thus it is unlikely that Asherah was understood as a goddess, especially one of the chief goddesses, in the areas of Israel, Judah, or Phoenicia during the Iron Age.

The goddess Ashtarte is also distinctly spelled Ashtoreth in the books of Judges, 1 Samuel, and 1 and 2 Kings. In all of these contexts, (plural, Ashtaroth) is specifically mentioned as a pagan goddess, and often alongside other pagan deities. Thus, a distinction between Ashtarte and the Asherah is clearly made.

The description of varying religious practices from the Bible agrees with the archaeological and ancient textual evidence—at times there was rampant religious syncretism, such as the use of a sacred tree cult object called the Asherah at a shrine for Yahweh, but the Israelites did not create a goddess consort for Yahweh named Asherah. Because the Israelites were commanded never to make cult objects and to destroy any of those that they found, throughout the centuries prophets and leaders in ancient Israel spoke against these polytheistic practices, and led movements to destroy idols, temples, and altars in order to eliminate the worship of gods and goddesses such as Astarte.

When the men of the city arose early in the morning, behold, the altar of Baal was torn down, and the Asherah which was beside it was cut down (Judges 6:28).

(30) Ba'al Hadad, God of Canaan
(Ba'al Statue and Altar)

Date: 15th century BC

Discovered: Hazor (Tell el Qedah, Israel)

Period: Conquest

Keywords: Ba'al; Hadad; god; idol; altar

Bible Passages: Joshua 11:10-11; Judges 2:1-13; 6:25; Deuteronomy 12:3; Numbers 33:52

Ba'al Hadad, the king of the gods in the pantheon of Canaan, was a storm god often depicted in an action pose wielding a lightning bolt, similar to Zeus. Many statues, figurines, stelae, and altars representing and dedicated to Ba'al Hadad have been discovered in Canaan, especially in the period from approximately 1800–1100 BC during the time of the patriarchs, Joshua, and the judges.

A stone statue probably carved about the 15th century BC in Canaan represents Ba'al Hadad in striding pose and originally with a bolt of lightning.[38] While Ba'al means "lord" and is not a proper name, the title was often used to refer to the chief god of the pantheon. In the Hebrew Bible, this god is always referred to simply as Baal, while usage of the plural refers to other pagan male deities.

---

[38] Preserved depictions of Ba'al Hadad allow visualization of what the original statue would have looked like.

Many of the Israelites adopted the worship of Ba'al Hadad, especially in the judges period and the divided kingdom. However, originally the Israelites had been commanded to destroy these symbols of pagan worship, and evidence of ritual desecration has been discovered archaeologically.

At Hazor, excavation of one of these pagan temples showed the full extent of the destruction by the Israelites. The temple had been burned, and heads of idols had been cut off, including a basalt statue of Ba'al Hadad.[39] The cutting off of the heads and hands was not only physical destruction of an idol, but it symbolically depicted them as powerless false gods.

You shall tear down their altars and smash their standing stones and burn their [Asherah poles] with fire, and you shall cut down the engraved images of their gods (Deuteronomy 12:3).

---

[39] An elaborate stone altar from the Late Bronze Age, cut from basalt and dedicated to the god Ba'al Hadad, was also discovered at Hazor. Gideon was instructed to destroy the altar of Baal that belonged to his father.

(31) DESTRUCTION AND SETTLEMENT OF DAN
(Collared-Rim Jars)

Date: 12th century BC
Discovered: Dan/Laish (Tell el Qadi, Israel)
Period: Judges
Keywords: pottery; Laish; migration
Bible Passage: Judges 18:7-29

When the Israelites settled in Canaan, their towns and cities came to be characterized by several features that are discernible in archaeology, including the four-room house, a lack of pig bones, no temples or idols, simple pit burials, circular settlement layouts, storage pits, and a distinctive type of pottery called a collared-rim storage jar.

Archaeological excavations at ancient Dan, located south of Mount Hermon and near sources of the Jordan River, uncovered a destruction of the Late Bronze II city in the early 12th century BC, followed by an immediate rebuilding and resettlement of the site. Among the discoveries from the rebuilt city were storage pits containing large ceramic jars with a distinctive collared rim. When the clay from these storage jars was examined through petrographic analysis, it was determined that these large jars had been manufactured elsewhere in Israel and then brought to the new city, suggesting that Dan had been resettled by outsiders who had attacked the previous city and displaced its residents.

This collared-rim storage jar was also a specific type of pottery made by Israelite potters, becoming common in the 13th century BC when Israel had developed its own unique material culture, and continuing into the time of the kingdoms of Israel and Judah. Therefore, the attackers and new settlers of Dan were able to be tentatively identified through archaeology as Israelite due to the distinctive pottery style and its origin.

According to the book of Judges, during the 12th century BC, the Israelite tribe of Dan was searching for a place to settle because they had been unable to establish themselves in Philistine territory. While searching, they decided upon an isolated city north of the Sea of Galilee, originally called Laish—an ancient city name also known from the Egyptian Execration Texts and the Karnak list of Pharaoh Thutmose III. The tribe of Dan attacked this city, destroyed it, and then resettled the area and named the city Dan after their tribe and patriarch, transforming it into an Israelite city for centuries.

> [They] came to Laish, to a people quiet and secure, and struck them with the edge of the sword, and they burned the city with fire...And they rebuilt the city and lived in it. They called the name of the city Dan (Judges 18:27-29).

(32) THE ARK AND THE PHILISTINES
(Izbet Sartah Ostracon)

Date: 11th century BC

Discovered: Ebenezer (Izbet Sartah, Israel)

Period: Judges

Keywords: ostracon; Hebrew; inscription; Ebenezer; Philistines

Bible Passage: 1 Samuel 4:1–7:2

An ancient Hebrew ostracon[40] was discovered in a grain silo at the archaeological site of Izbet Sartah, identified as the ancient town of Ebenezer, east of Aphek. This inscribed pottery sherd, designated the Izbet Sartah Ostracon, dates to about the

---

[40] *Ostracon/ostraca:* A pottery sherd containing writing, usually written using black carbon ink or inscribed into the piece of pottery.

11th century BC and contains a text of 5 lines with over 80 letters, including the ancient Hebrew alphabet.

Written using Proto-Canaanite characters read from left to right, the inscription demonstrates that alphabetic writing was known and practiced in Israel during the judges period and the time of Eli.[41] Because many of the letters in the inscription have faded and are extremely difficult to read, there are disputes about the content and purpose of the inscription. An alphabet is clearly visible, and the content of the other lines has been debated, but it appears to have been a practice tablet for someone learning to write or become a scribe. A few scholars claim the inscription is merely a mass of letters and random words for practice, while others interpret the allegedly random words as an actual donation inscription.

However, another proposed translation suggests that the text preserves a summarized version of the capture and return of the ark of the covenant in the 11th century BC. According to this translation the ostracon mentions movement of people from Aphek to Shiloh, then the Kittim (Philistines) taking something to Azor, then to the god Dagon at Ashdod, then to Gath, and finally the town of Kiriath-Jearim. Soldiers, the name Hophni, and a brother (perhaps Phineas) are also mentioned, and it seems that Hophni had died.[42]

This translation matches the route and names recorded in the book of Samuel, when the Philistines had left Aphek, defeated the Israelites, then proceeded to Shiloh to take the ark of the covenant before eventually returning it. If this translation is correct, then the text would be a contemporary summarized account of a passage in the book of Samuel. However, at the very least the ostracon demonstrates literacy even in villages of Israel during the judges period.

> *Now the Philistines took the ark of God and brought it from Ebenezer to Ashdod. Then the Philistines took the ark of God and brought it to the house of Dagon (1 Samuel 5:1-2).*

---

[41] Hebrew was written and read from right to left during the kingdom period and later, but it appears that earlier in the judges period and before it could perhaps be written and read in either direction.

[42] Phineas, the brother of Hophni, is not mentioned by name on the ostracon.

CHAPTER 4

THE UNITED MONARCHY OF SAUL, DAVID, AND SOLOMON

(Samuel–Kings)

In the 20th century, mounting cynicism about the historicity of David and the kingdom of Solomon eventually resulted in claims that David never existed and Solomon was merely a tribal chieftain rather than the monarch of a vast kingdom. However, an artifact then surfaced that mentioned the royal house of David, and discoveries at various archaeological sites indicated that Solomon ruled a vast and powerful kingdom, showing the narratives about the monarchy to be historically accurate.

After being led by judges for over 300 years, the Israelites were determined to be like the other nations and finally demanded a king, ushering in the period of the United Monarchy in which all 12 tribes of Israel would be ruled as a nation by one man. Saul was selected as the first king to rule over all the tribes, although his reign was tumultuous and marked by war with the Philistines, including the famous duel between David and the giant Goliath.

Because Saul failed to follow and honor God, the prophet Samuel anointed David as the next king even while Saul still held power. Eventually, Saul was overtaken by the Philistines in battle on Mount Gilboa, and he fell on his own sword.

David replaced Saul as king around 1010 BC and began a dynasty that would continually rule for approximately 423 years during the archaeological period known as the Iron Age II (ca. 1000–587 BC). First reigning from Hebron, David conquered Jerusalem seven years later, establishing the capital there and beginning preparations for the temple.

In about 970 BC, Solomon, son of David and Bathsheba, became king while his father was near death. Famous for his wisdom and wealth, Solomon built the temple in Jerusalem, constructed new fortifications around the country, expanded trade, and wrote wisdom literature, but he also adopted pagan religious practices as a result of marrying foreign wives.

The artifacts in this section, which were found in Israel, Philistia, and Ammon, both illuminate and corroborate the period of the United Monarchy.

(33) Eshbaal and Saul
(Ishbaal Son of Beda Jar)

Date: 1000 BC

Discovered: Shaarayim (?) (Khirbet Qeiyafa, Israel)

Period: United Monarchy

Keywords: pottery; Ishbaal; Eshbaal; Ish-bosheth; ostracon

Bible Passages: 2 Samuel 2:8; 1 Chronicles 8:33

During excavations of an Iron Age building at Khirbet Qeiyafa, an inscribed storage jar was discovered on the floor underneath debris. The inscription consists of 15 letters in an ancient script similar to older Canaanite inscriptions, but distinct from later Phoenician, while the language is considered Hebrew. The archaeological context, the form of the letters, and the name on the jar places the date around 1000 BC. The inscription reads "Ishbaal son of Beda," with a debated preceding word that has been suggested as "expiation." Based on the finds at Qeiyafa, the site was an Israelite town, perhaps Sha'arayim, and therefore the person mentioned on the jar would likely be an Israelite.

According to the books of Chronicles and Samuel, King Saul had a son named Ishbaal or Eshbaal who lived around this time, while the name Beda is yet unknown from any other texts.[43] Although this appears to have been a different Ishbaal than the son of Saul, it does demonstrate that the name was in use in Israelite circles only around 1000 BC, perhaps losing popularity due to the failure of Ishbaal and the Baal (lord) theophoric element.

> *Saul became the father of Jonathan, Malchi-shua, Abinadab and Eshbaal (1 Chronicles 8:33).*

---

[43] The name *Ish-bosheth* in 2 Samuel appears to be an intentional modification of the name *Eth-Baal* in order to remove reference to the pagan god Baal.

(34) The Mysterious Piym
(Inscribed PYM Weight)

Date: 10th century BC (?)

Discovered: Gezer, Israel

Period: United Monarchy

Keywords: weight; piym; Gezer; measurement

Bible Passage: 1 Samuel 13:21

A unique passage in the book of 1 Samuel described how no blacksmiths could be found in Israel, so the people went to the Philistines to sharpen their tools. But an unknown and mysterious word *PYM* caused confusion about the meaning and interpretation of the narrative.[44]

For centuries, Bible translators had no idea what the word *PYM* meant since it appeared nowhere else in the Old Testament and no ancient lexicons had translated its meaning. However, archaeological excavations at Gezer in the early 1900s uncovered a stone weight inscribed in ancient Hebrew script with the word *PYM*

---

[44] *PYM* is variously transliterated as piym, pim, and payim.

and the mystery was solved. When analyzed, it was understood that the piym weight was an ancient stone-weight denomination equivalent to about 7.6 grams or two-thirds of a shekel, and this was the price in weight of silver to sharpen the tools.[45]

Prior to the introduction of standardized currency in minted coins, silver or other precious metals were typically weighed out on one side of a scale, with a stone weight or weights on the other side of the scale. Numerous examples of the piym weight have now been discovered in the area of ancient Israel. Although the weight was apparently common at one time in Israelite history, it fell out of use during the Divided Kingdom period of Israel and Judah and was no longer known by the time of the Intertestamental Period.[46] Since the book of Samuel used this word that was lost to history, it demonstrates that the author lived in the time of ancient Israel.

> *The fee was a piym for the plowshare and for the sickle and for the sharp pitchfork and for the axes and to fix the oxgoads (1 Samuel 13:21 AUTHOR'S TRANSLATION).*

---

[45] These stone weights were rounded and typically about 15 mm in diameter, with the name of the weight inscribed on the top side. There were different types of shekels, but the standard shekel in ancient Israel, although it could vary slightly, weighed approximately 11.4 grams.

[46] The Intertestamental Period, or 400 years of silence, was the time between the prophet Malachi and John the Baptizer, or roughly the period between the Old Testament and New Testament.

(35) LETTER ABOUT A KING
(Qeiyafa Ostracon)

Date: 1000 BC

Discovered: Khirbet Qeiyafa (Shaarayim?, Israel)

Period: United Monarchy

Keywords: ostracon; Hebrew; letter; Elah; king

Bible Passages: Joshua 15:36; 1 Samuel 17:52; 2 Samuel 11:14-15; 1 Chronicles 4:31

A letter written in ancient Hebrew and dating to about 1000 BC was discovered at the site of Khirbet Qeiyafa, known as the Elah Fortress.[47] Situated at the border

---

[47] Qeiyafa is a 2.3 hectare (about five acres) site in the Shephelah (Judean foothills) on the north side of the Elah Valley, about 20 km southwest of Jerusalem. It was an Israelite fortress dated by pottery and radiocarbon tests to approximately 1050–970 BC. Excavations at the site uncovered no pig bones, no idols, and pottery distinct from the styles of the nearby Philistine cities, which, along with the Hebrew letter, conclusively demonstrated that it was an Israelite fortress.

between ancient Israel and Philistia, the fortress overlooked the Elah Valley where David defeated Goliath. Because of the two gates found at this fortress, the excavators suggest that it was the town of Sha'arayim (meaning "two gates"), which appears in Joshua, Samuel, and Chronicles. The letter was written using black carbon ink on a square sherd of pottery (an ostracon), and it is also read left to right and appears with the Proto-Canaanite letters similar to those found on the Izbet Sartah Ostracon, which differ from the standard Hebrew alphabet known from inscriptions in Israel and Judah during the period of the Divided Kingdom.

This letter from the time of King David, found at the Elah Fortress, is significant not only because it further demonstrates literacy of the Israelites and early usage of written Hebrew, but the content informs us of historical context that matches descriptions of the time in the Bible.

Although the ink is faded and certain letters are difficult to read, the text of five lines mentions a command, serving God, and the king. Because the fortress was Israelite and the language of the letter was Hebrew, it demonstrates that there was a king in Israel at that time, that the kingdom extended far beyond merely the area of Jerusalem, that Israelites, including their king, were literate and wrote letters, and that the Israelite border with the Philistines was at the Elah Valley at the time of David—all of which is also recorded in the books of Samuel and Chronicles.

> *Now in the morning David wrote a letter to Joab and sent it by the hand of Uriah... "Place Uriah in the front line of the fiercest battle and withdraw from him" (2 Samuel 11:14-15).*

(36) Goliath of Gath
(The Goliath Ostracon)

Date: 10th or 9th century BC

Discovered: Gath, Philistia (Tel es-Safi, Israel)

Period: United Monarchy

Keywords: Gath; ostracon; Philistine; Goliath

Bible Passages: 1 Samuel 17:4-52; 21:9; 2 Samuel 21:19-22

The Gath Ostracon or Goliath Ostracon is an inscribed piece of pottery from the 10th or 9th century BC that was discovered during excavations at the ancient Philistine city of Gath. Analysis indicates that the inscription represents two names or a name and a word. The first name appears to be a form of the name Goliath, although scholars differ on the exact interpretation of the letters and the translation of the text.

However, the inscription comes from the city of Goliath and his descendants, not long after the wars between David and the giants of Gath, and it records a Philistine or Aegean name "Goliath" (or one etymologically equivalent), demonstrating that Philistines did live in Gath and that the name "Goliath" was used in that city during the time of the United Monarchy of Israel in the beginning of the Iron Age II.

In ancient Aegean culture, the greatest warriors and heroes of their opposing armies participated in a one-on-one battle called monomaxia, which could decide the fate of the battle. Achilles and Hector, recorded in the *Iliad* and depicted in ancient artwork, is the most famous example, but numerous others are known from ancient Greek literature. These duels were fought to show superiority, the winning side, and strike fear into the losing side, which could easily turn the tide of battle. The tradition seems to have emerged from ancient Aegean culture and continued on for hundreds of years.

When David fought a duel against Goliath, champion of the Philistines who were of Aegean descent, the two warriors engaged in this *monomaxia* single combat. After David defeated and killed Goliath, which seemed almost impossible, this panicked the Philistines and sent them into retreat.[48]

> *A champion came out from the armies of the Philistines named Goliath, from Gath (1 Samuel 17:4).*

---

[48] Although many Bible translations give the height of Goliath as six cubits and a span (about nine feet nine) following the Masoretic text, the Dead Sea Scrolls and the Septuagint, more than 1,000 years older than the Masoretic text, state the height of Goliath as four cubits and a span (about six feet nine). This shorter height was still considerably taller than the average man at the time (approximately five feet five), meaning Goliath would have towered over David. A height for Goliath just under seven feet tall is also in agreement with archaeological findings for the tallest known skeletal remains of humans in that area from ancient times.

(37) Agriculture and the Calendar
(Gezer Calendar)

Date: 10th century BC

Discovered: Gezer, Israel

Period: United Monarchy

Keywords: Gezer; calendar; Hebrew; agriculture; literacy

Bible Passages: Exodus 23:14-16; Numbers 13:20; Ruth 1:22; 1 Samuel 8:2; 1 Kings 14:1

At the site of ancient Gezer, west of Jerusalem and northwest of Bethlehem, a limestone tablet inscribed in ancient Hebrew was found during excavations in 1908. Dating to the 10th century BC, at the beginning of the United Monarchy period and just after the time of the judges, it was for many years the oldest Hebrew inscription discovered through archaeology.

The tablet was designated the Gezer Calendar because it describes 12 months of agricultural activities during the year. The text is composed of 7 lines read left to right, followed by a name at the bottom of the tablet. Specifically, the inscription is translated as "two months of harvest, two months of sowing, two months of late growth, one month of cutting flax, one month of barley, one month of measuring, two months of pruning the field, one month of fruit harvest."

The Hebrew name Abiyah ("my father is Yahweh") appears on the tablet, perhaps signed by the author, and is a name known from books such as Samuel, Kings, and Chronicles.

Because the text mentions agricultural duties associated with the months, one interpretation suggests that it was related to the collection of taxes. Another interpretation is that it was a folk song, but there is no parallel evidence in biblical texts or Hebrew inscriptions that indicate it would have been related to taxes or that it was a song.

However, both the front and the back of the tablet show repeated use. The tablet was inscribed, erased, and inscribed again, indicating that it may have been a practice tablet for scribal training. Regardless of its identity as either an official inscription or a practice tablet, the Gezer Calendar reveals that the ancient Israelites during the early monarchy period used a 12-month calendar, and that the economy of the kingdom was based around agriculture.

This 12-month Israelite calendar and the various associated agricultural activities can also be reconstructed from many passages throughout the Old Testament, corroborating the use of a 12-month calendar and the general agricultural cycles recorded in the Bible. Although the Gezer Calendar does not name the months, the month names known from the Old Testament were: (1) Abib, (2) Ziv, (3) Sivan, (4) unknown, (5) unknown, (6) Elul, (7) Ethanim, (8) Bul, (9) Chislev, (10) Teveth, (11) Shevat, and (12) Adar.

Further, the presence of the name Abijah on the Gezer Calendar is archaeological attestation of the use of that name in the 10th century BC, which is also the time period according to the Bible when Abijah was a common name in Israel and Judah.

> *Naomi returned, and with her Ruth the Moabite, her daughter-in-law, who returned from the land of Moab. And they came to Bethlehem at the beginning of barley harvest (Ruth 1:22).*

(38) THE ROYAL HOUSE OF DAVID
(Tel Dan Stele)

Date: 9th century BC

Discovered: Dan, Israel

Period: United Monarchy and Divided Kingdom

Keywords: David; stele; king; Aram; Jehoram; Ahaz; Hazael; Ben-Hadad

Bible Passages: 2 Samuel 3:1-6; 1 Kings 12:19-26; 15:16-22; Psalm 122:5

As skepticism toward the Bible as a historically reliable document increased, many scholars eventually began to claim that David was a fictitious king since no ancient evidence had been discovered to corroborate his position as king or even his existence.

During excavations at ancient Dan in 1993, fragments of a 9th-century BC Aramean victory stele were discovered at the base of a wall on the edge of a plaza near the main city gate. Presumably, the stele would have been erected at the entrance to the city, and the stone monument is estimated to have originally been about 3.3 feet (1 m) tall and 19.6 inches (50 cm) wide. However, it was smashed in antiquity, probably by the Israelites when they regained power of the city.

Written in Aramaic, the recovered stele consists of 3 main fragments comprising 13 lines of text. Narrating victories, the inscription mentions Jehoram of Israel and Ahaziahu of Judah. Although the name of the Aramean king is not found on the known text, this king was probably Hazael of Aram or Ben-Hadad II of Aram, who are both recorded in the book of Kings as having waged war against Israel and were based at Damascus about 30 miles (48 km) to the northeast.

In the context of these kings of Israel and Judah, on line 9 of the stele the "house of David" (*byt dwd*) is noted as the original ruling house of the Israelite kingdom. The "house of" formula was common in the ancient Near East as a designation for a founder of a royal house, which demonstrates that David was known as the king of Israel and first in the dynasty even by the neighboring Arameans.

After analysis, the stele was confirmed to be the earliest known reference to King David, the Israelite monarch. The monumental inscription was carved into basalt and placed at Dan by the Arameans after they conquered the Israelites and subdued the city as early as 870 BC.

This phrase "house of David" is also found in the books of Samuel, Kings, Chronicles, Psalms, Isaiah, Jeremiah, and Zechariah. The presence of David on a victory stele of the Arameans, enemies of Israel, means that it could not have been propaganda about a legendary king, indicating that the David referred to on the stele was a historical king.

The inscription "house of David" is extremely significant due to its ancient attestation of David as king of Israel, which was disputed by many scholars prior to the discovery of the Tel Dan Stele. Subsequent to its discovery, the 9th-century Mesha Stele was reevaluated and also found that it, too, had the phrase "house of David" referring to the royal descendants of King David.

Now there was a long war between the house of Saul and the house of David (2 Samuel 3:1).

(39) Kings and Crowns
(Ammonite King Statue)

Date: 8th century BC

Discovered: Rabbah, Ammon (Amman, Jordan)

Period: United Monarchy and Divided Kingdom

Keywords: crown; king; Ammon; David; Solomon

Bible Passages: 2 Samuel 1:10; 12:28-30; 2 Kings 11:12; 1 Chronicles 20:1-2; 2 Chronicles 23:11; Psalm 21:3; Song of Solomon 3:11

During the time of the United Monarchy, the kings of Israel adopted the tradition of wearing crowns, beginning with Saul. However, two main types of crowns were used—one was a diadem type of crown, which was small and could be worn on any occasion, while the other was a large helmet type of crown, which was ceremonial.

When the forces of David captured the city of Rabbah, the capital of Ammon, David took the crown of their king for himself and placed it on his head. This crown was described as weighing a talent, made of gold, and decorated with a precious stone. According to ancient sources, the weight of a talent was approximately 75 pounds, which demonstrates that this was an impractical ceremonial crown that could not be worn under normal circumstances.

The discovery of a crowned king statue from Rabbah, Ammon, carved from limestone, originally painted, and dating to the 8th century BC, demonstrates this type of heavy, cone-shaped, ceremonial crown that David acquired from a king of that period and region. This helmet-type crown also resembles those worn by kings of many other nations in the ancient Near East and Egypt, and the crown type used for statues and depictions of gods.[49]

According to the books of Samuel, Chronicles, Psalms, and Song of Solomon, it appears that both David and Solomon used this type of crown, and it may have been handed down to the subsequent kings in the dynasty, although this helmet crown is not mentioned again in the context of other kings of Israel and Judah.

> *David gathered all the people and went to Rabbah, fought against it and captured it. Then he took the crown of their king from his head; and its weight was a talent of gold, and in it was a precious stone; and it was placed on David's head (2 Samuel 12:29-30).*

---

[49] The helmet type of crown was called *atarah*, while the diadem type of crown was called *nezer* and is mentioned later during the 9th century BC in association with the crowning of Jehoash of Judah.

(40) CASTING LOTS
(Israelite Astragali)

Date: 11th century BC

Discovered: Tel Hadar, Israel

Period: United Monarchy

Keywords: lots; purim; astragali; divination; Urim and Thummim; dice

Bible Passages: Exodus 28:30; Leviticus 8:8-10; Numbers 27:21; Joshua 18:6-10; Judges 20:9; 1 Samuel 14:41-42; 28:6; 1 Chronicles 24:5-7; Esther 3:7-9; 9:24; Proverbs 16:33; Acts 1:26

Astragali, also known as lots and a sort of precursor to dice, were animal talus bones (lower part of the ankle joint) used throughout the ancient world as objects in a religious ritual or as game pieces. Most commonly used in a decision ritual attempting to discover the will of God or gods, which in modern times is often referred to as cleromancy or divination, the six-sided pieces were cast and then read according to their markings or distinctive sides.

The ways in which the astragali were modified or decorated varied, but numbers, letters, or symbols could be carved on different sides. The outcome of the cast would then be read and interpreted as a divine decision, absent human interference.

In the ancient Near East and the Mediterranean region, astragali were almost always made from the bones of sheep or goats, and most discoveries of astragali groups are easily identifiable. Found in archaeological contexts from the Chalcolithic to the Roman period, astragali remained essentially standardized for millennia except for specific modifications such as carving, drilling, grinding, or polishing.

Casting lots is mentioned several times throughout the Bible, and significant numbers of astragali used in rituals have been found at many ancient sites in Israel, including a collection of 684 from the 10th century BC found at Megiddo, one of the main urban centers in the time of Solomon, attesting to the widespread use of lots in Israelite society. The Urim and Thummim of the high priest may even have been a special type of object similar to lots, as a few verses indicate that these were used to determine the will of the Lord.

Passages in the Bible record how the Israelites used lots, which would have been either astragali, special stones, or a similar object to determine decisions regarding land inheritance, deciding on war plans, settling disputes, exposing sinners, designating guard duty, and determining priestly service. However, the decisions were supposed to be from Yahweh, not by random chance or a pagan god.

> *The lot is cast into the lap, but its every decision is from [Yahweh] (Proverbs 16:33).*

(41) THE GOLD OF OPHIR
(Tell Qasile Ophir Inscription)

Date: 8th century BC

Discovered: Tell Qasile, Israel

Period: United Monarchy

Keywords: Ophir; Solomon; gold; ostracon

Bible Passages: 1 Kings 9:27-28; 10:11-22; 22:48; 2 Chronicles 8:18; Psalm 45:9; Ecclesiastes 2:8

One of the places where Solomon obtained his wealth and gold was called Ophir, which was a land of unspecified location renowned for its resources and mentioned in the books of Kings, Chronicles, Job, Psalms, and Isaiah. This "gold of Ophir" seems to have been a major source of the riches of King Solomon and a material used in decorating both the temple and his palace in Jerusalem. King Jehoshaphat of Judah also attempted an expedition to Ophir in the 9th century BC, but the expedition failed because the ships were destroyed.

A Hebrew inscription from the 8th century BC mentions the "gold of Ophir for Beth-Horon…30 shekels" and was probably a donation receipt. The text, from an inscribed pottery sherd, was discovered at Tell Qasile on the Mediterranean coast in the area of modern Tel Aviv. The inscription confirms the existence of Ophir and that it was a source of gold for the Israelite kings such as Solomon and those who followed. Ophir was reached by ship and probably located along the eastern coast of Africa, perhaps around Somalia or Mozambique.

> *They went to Ophir and took four hundred and twenty talents of gold from there, and brought it to King Solomon (1 Kings 9:28).*

CHAPTER 5

SHATTERED KINGDOMS
(Kings–Chronicles)

The prevailing view about the accounts of the divided kingdoms of Israel and Judah in the Bible are that these books were propaganda written by the official scribes of the kingdom of Judah to give the people a history, legitimize their government, and promote the worship of Yahweh according to the views of the priestly class, who had allegedly invented this new religion and imposed it on the formerly polytheistic Israelites.

However, the archaeological sources from this period are so vast and coincide so well with the biblical narratives that it is an untenable position to claim that books such as Kings and Chronicles are propaganda and pseudohistory. The artifact discoveries alone indicate a degree of historical attestation unparalleled for national texts of that era.

The split of the United Monarchy into the separate kingdoms of Israel and Judah occurred in about 931 BC when Jeroboam, the former general, rebelled against Rehoboam who was the son of Solomon and heir to the throne. The northern tribes followed Jeroboam, who established his royal residence at Shechem, while the tribes of Judah and Benjamin continued under the rule of Rehoboam with the capital at Jerusalem.

During this Divided Kingdom period, the north was heavily influenced by foreign nations, adopted many pagan deities and practices, and eventually the kingdom of Israel was destroyed and dispersed by the Assyrians in 722 BC. The kingdom of Judah also struggled with polytheism and pagan practices, but many of the kings and leaders followed God and observed the Law of Moses. As the Assyrian Empire expanded, Judah was also attacked in 701 BC by Sennacherib, but Jerusalem did not fall.

However, foreign powers continued to exert influence, as the Egyptians under Pharaoh Necho II controlled Judah briefly, appointing Jehoiakim as king. Soon after, in 605 BC, the Babylonians subdued Judah as a vassal kingdom, then finally destroyed Jerusalem and the temple in 587 BC after a rebellion, ending the period of the monarchy.

The artifacts from the Divided Kingdom section, which were found in Israel, Moab, Ammon, and Assyria, illustrate the narratives in the books of Kings, Chronicles, Isaiah, Jeremiah, and the minor prophets, while also demonstrating the historical accuracy of the texts through external archaeological evidence.

(42) Pharaoh Shishak
(Shoshenq I Megiddo Stele)

Date: 10th century BC

Discovered: Megiddo, Israel

Period: Divided Kingdom

Keywords: Shishak; Shoshenq; Megiddo; Jeroboam

Bible Passages: 1 Kings 14:25-26; 2 Chronicles 12:2-9

This fragment of a victory stele, found at Megiddo, contains the cartouche of Pharaoh Shoshenq I (Shishak). The fragment was discovered during excavations and corresponds to a destruction layer from the late 10th century BC.

According to Egyptian records and a list of cities displayed at the Bubastite Portal in the Karnak Temple, Pharaoh Shoshenq I campaigned against Israel and Judah ca. 925 BC. Megiddo is specifically noted, as are several other cities of Israel and Judah, including Taanach, Beth-Shean, Rehob, Arad, while either the king or capital of Judah is also mentioned. Archaeological excavations also found that several cities were destroyed in the 10th century BC at the time of Jeroboam, Rehoboam, and Shoshenq I.

Why would Shoshenq I campaign against Israel and Jeroboam if previously Jeroboam had fled to Egypt and stayed there for years, perhaps even working in the royal court? Perhaps Shoshenq I had made a deal with Jeroboam requiring tribute or vassal status for his aid, but Jeroboam failed to honor that agreement and thus incurred the wrath of the pharaoh.

The vast amount of treasure that Pharaoh Shishak took from Jerusalem, recorded in 1 Kings 14:25-26, also appears to coincide with the financial situation in Egypt following the end of the reign of Shoshenq I. Once he returned to Egypt, Shoshenq I began significant temple building projects at Thebes, Karnak, and El-Hiba.

The son and successor of Shoshenq I, Osorkon I, came to power about two years after the end of the Israel and Judah campaign. Osorkon I spent enormous amounts of gold and silver on the temples of Egypt within the early years of his reign, and the country was extremely prosperous during his time as king. If his father, Shoshenq I, had taken the treasure of Jerusalem back to Egypt, this would account for the ability to spend immense amounts of gold and silver on temples and improve the overall financial situation of Egypt.

The locations recorded on the Karnak campaign list, the destroyed cities in Israel and Judah, the victory stele of Shoshenq I at Megiddo, and the immense spending and prosperity in the reign of Osorkon I demonstrate that Shoshenq I campaigned against Israel and Judah at the time of Jeroboam and Rehoboam, and indicate that immense wealth was taken back to Egypt after the siege of Jerusalem.

Now it happened in the fifth year of King Rehoboam, that Shishak the king of Egypt came up against Jerusalem (1 Kings 14:25).

(43) KING JEROBOAM
(Seal of Jeroboam)

Date: 10th century BC

Discovered: Megiddo, Israel

Period: Divided Kingdom

Keywords: Megiddo; Jeroboam; seal

Bible Passages: 1 Kings 11:40–12:33; 2 Kings 14:23–15:1; 23:15; Hosea 1:1; Amos 1:1; 7:9-11

A seal with the Hebrew inscription "belonging to Shema, servant of Jeroboam" was excavated at Megiddo in the area of the gatehouse or palace of the late 10th century BC where it had likely been kept with other seals for official use. This seal, made of jasper, was decorated with a carved lion and painted on either side of the lion with an ankh and palm tree. Originally it was mounted on a ring of metal, but this may have been removed or ruined in antiquity when the city was attacked and destroyed by Pharaoh Shoshenq I.

After excavations around 1905, it was lost in Istanbul or on its way to Istanbul, but not before a photograph was taken and an accurate cast was made. Although some scholars have suggested the seal is from the 8th century BC, the stratigraphic evidence indicates the seal is from the 10th century BC and the reign of King Jeroboam I, the former warrior who became king (ca. 931–910 BC).[50] Jeroboam son of Nebat had rebelled against Solomon, fled to Egypt, returned after Rehoboam was crowned, and was soon made king by the northern tribes, becoming first king of the northern kingdom of Israel.[51]

> *It came about when all Israel heard that Jeroboam had returned, that they sent and called him to the assembly and made him king over all Israel. None but the tribe of Judah followed the house of David (1 Kings 12:20).*

---

[50] Jeroboam II ruled the northern kingdom of Israel from about 793–753 BC, overlapping with Uzziah in Judah. The prophets Hosea, Amos, and perhaps Joel served during his reign.

[51] Jeroboam I also erected "illegal" massive horned stone altars with golden calf idols in Dan and Bethel. The golden calf idols were probably melted down in ancient times and reused, and the altar at Bethel was "ground to dust" according to the book of Kings, but remnants of the horned altar at Dan were discovered, including one of the large stone horns.

(44) THE GOD MILCOM
(Amman Citadel Inscription)

Date: 9th century BC

Discovered: Rabbath-Ammon (Amman, Jordan)

Period: Divided Kingdom

Keywords: Milcom; Molech; Topheth; sacrifice; Ammonite

Bible Passages: Leviticus 20:1-5; Deuteronomy 12:29-31; 1 Kings 11:5-7; 2 Kings 23:13; Jeremiah 49:1

The Amman Citadel Inscription is an Ammonite text of the 9th century BC found at the citadel of ancient Rabbath-Ammon, capital of the kingdom of Ammon.[52] Inscribed with eight lines of alphabetic script in stone, the plaque appears to have been regarded as an official document recording the words of the god Milcom (or Milkom), threats of death, the citadel, and possibly a temple. It has been interpreted as an oracle or commands from Milcom, primary god of the Ammonites.

In the 10th century, Solomon began following other gods that his neighbors worshipped, such as Milcom, the chief god of the pantheon in Ammon, which the book of Kings referred to as a detestable idol. This deity is also mentioned as being worshipped by some people in Judah at the time of Josiah and Jeremiah during the 7th century BC, and appears to be linked to the Topheth ("furnace" or "pyre," cf. Isaiah 30:33) in the valley of Hinnom where fire sacrifice of children was apparently occurring.

---

[52] The inscription is carved on a piece of limestone about 6.5 cm tall and 5 cm wide. It was discovered in 1961 and published in 1968.

Because of the possible links to human sacrifice by burning and the similarity of the names, the child sacrifices to Molech involving fire, which were prohibited in Leviticus, conceivably refer to the same deity or the same type of sacrificial practice.[53]

Outside of Rabbath-Ammon, a large stone altar from the Bronze Age was discovered and excavated that included hundreds of burned human bone fragments and a cylinder seal depicting human sacrifice. This human sacrifice may have been associated with the cult of Milcom, the primary deity of the region, and it persisted for centuries into the time of the kingdom of Judah.

> *The high places which were before Jerusalem, which were on the right of the mount of destruction which Solomon the king of Israel had built...for Milcom the abomination of the sons of Ammon, the king defiled (2 Kings 23:13).*

---

[53] Texts from Ebla, Ugarit, and Mari also mention a deity *mlk*, which appears to have been a god of the underworld and probably the same as Molech. At the Topheth of Carthage, a massive cemetery filled with the burnt bones of infants and children, and inscriptions and artwork on stele, have been discovered that also appear to link a deity or type of sacrifice called Molech to human sacrifice by fire.

(45) Mesha of Moab
(The Mesha Stele)

Date: 9th century BC

Discovered: Dibon, Moab (Dhiban, Jordan)

Period: Divided Kingdom

Keywords: Mesha; Moab; Omri; Dibon; Chemosh; David; Jehoram; Yahweh

Bible Passages: 1 Kings 11:7; 2 Kings 3:4-27

The Mesha Stele or Moabite Stone is a 9th-century BC stone victory monument composed of 34 inscribed lines, commissioned by King Mesha and discovered in Moab. The stele is carved basalt from about 835 BC and measures 4.07 feet (1.24 m) tall, up to 2.6 feet (79 cm) wide, and about 1.2 feet (36 cm) thick.

The inscription, which is the longest known in the Moabite language, relates the successful victory of Mesha over Israel and Judah after his rebellion and refusal to continue tribute. The text names Omri as a king of Israel in the 9th century BC, Mesha as a king of Moab in the 9th century BC, the tribe of Gad, locations such as Ataroth and Dibon, Chemosh the chief god of Moab, recounts the rebellion by Moab during the reign of Jehoram from the Moabite perspective, has the earliest known Semitic inscription mentioning Yahweh, and even seems to contain an early reference to the "house of David."

The stele was discovered in the ruins of Dhiban in 1868 by a bedouin who subsequently showed it to a missionary and scholars living in the area. Unfortunately, the bedouins looted and then smashed the stele during negotiations for sale, but the recovered pieces were eventually sent to the Louvre Museum and reconstructed with the help of a paper squeeze that had been taken before it was broken.

Translation revealed the Moabite perspective on a conflict also recorded in the book of Kings, plus additional information about events before and after, and insight into the religion of Moab. The inscription begins with the lineage of Mesha and recounts how he constructed a sanctuary to the god Chemosh. Lines 5-8 describe how Omri, king of Israel, had oppressed Moab and taken the land of Medeba, continuing through half the reign of his descendant (Jehoram). Line 3 mentions Chemosh, the main god of the Moabites also mentioned in the book of Kings. Lines 11, 16, and 17 indicate that the Moabites exterminated inhabitants of captured cities as a dedicatory sacrifice to the god Chemosh, which is consistent with the Hebrew Bible account about Mesha offering his son as a sacrifice in order to appease his god Chemosh and inspire his followers.

Line 31 is fragmentary, but using a combination of detailed examination of the stele, a paper impression of the inscription taken just after the time of discovery but before it was smashed, and an early drawing of the stele based on the impression and the fragments, analysis indicates that the "house of David" is mentioned near the end of the text.[54]

The remainder of the stele recounts Moabite victories over Israel and details how Mesha led a successful campaign against cities in Israel, substantiating the claim in the book of Kings that the land conquered by Omri was taken back by the Moabites in the days of Mesha.

> *Now Mesha king of Moab was a sheep breeder, and used to pay the king of Israel…But when Ahab died, the king of Moab rebelled against the king of Israel (2 Kings 3:4-5).*

---

[54] Recently, a few scholars claimed that instead of "house of David" (*BT DWD*) the Mesha stele inscription mentioned "Balak" (*BLQ*), the Moabite king mentioned in the book of Numbers, based on the presence of the letter *B*, an unreadable second letter, ignoring the partial *D* at the beginning of *DWD*, and an inventive hypothesis about Balak constructed through mere speculation.

(46) Elisha on Pottery
(Rehov Elisha Ostracon)

Date: 9th century BC
Discovered: Rehov, Israel
Period: Divided Kingdom
Keywords: Elisha; Rehov; ostracon
Bible Passage: 1 Kings 19:15-19

An ancient Hebrew ostracon that reads "belonging to Elisha" was discovered in a 9th-century BC house during excavations in the ruins of ancient Rehov. Using a reddish ink and writing in the archaic Hebrew script, the owner marked his property.

Although the prophet who succeeded Elijah was named Elisha, lived in the 9th century BC, and was born several miles away in Abel Meholah, the Rehov house in which the ostracon was found is almost certainly not the house of Elisha the prophet, as it was found full of idols and pagan altars, which the prophet preached against.

However, the ostracon does attest to use of the name Elisha in the 9th century BC kingdom of Israel and in the general area of where Elisha was born and lived.

Elisha the son of Shaphat of Abel-meholah you shall anoint as prophet in your place (1 Kings 19:16).

(47) Ahab and His Army
(Kurkh Stele of Shalmaneser III)

Date: 852 BC

Discovered: Khurk (west of Bismil, Turkey)

Period: Divided Kingdom

Keywords: Ahab; Jezreel; Shalmaneser III; chariot; Qarqar

Bible Passage: 1 Kings 20:13–21:1

The Kurkh Stele of Shalmaneser III, commissioned by a king of Assyria who reigned approximately 859–824 BC, was one of two monolithic Assyrian stelae found in the town of Kurkh in modern southeast Turkey, west of Lake Van. Part of a pair belonging to Shalmaneser III and his father Ashurnasirpal II, the monolith depicts Shalmaneser III and commemorates his successful campaigns.[55]

Among other battles, the cuneiform text recounts the battle of Qarqar, which occurred in about 853 BC, and mentions king "Ahab the Israelite" with his contribution of 2,000 chariots and 10,000 soldiers to the opposing, defeated coalition of 12 kings. The chariot force of Ahab is the largest of any in the coalition, demonstrating his military might and his emphasis on using chariots in battle.

---

[55] This stele of Shalmaneser III was carved from a block of limestone about 2.21 meters tall, 87 centimeters wide, and 23 centimeters thick. There is text on the front, sides, and back of the stone.

While this particular event is not recorded in the Bible, Ahab was a wealthy and powerful king who was involved in numerous chariot battles during his reign. Evidence from archaeological excavations at Jezreel also indicates that he maintained a large portion of his chariot corps at this royal fortress city with a rectangular  fortification comprised of walls about 860 feet long and 470 feet wide, where a huge enclosed courtyard was discovered that could accommodate thousands of his chariots.

> *[Ahab] king of Israel went out and struck the horses and chariots, and killed the Arameans with a great slaughter... Then Ben-hadad came out to him, and he took him up into the chariot (1 Kings 20:21,33).*

(48) Queen Jezebel
(Seal of Jezebel)

Date: 9th century BC

Discovered: Unknown, Israel

Period: Divided Kingdom

Keywords: Jezebel; Ahab; Phoenician; seal

Bible Passage: 1 Kings 16:29-31

An inscribed and decorated stone seal with the name Jezebel, found at an unknown site in Israel, was eventually donated to a museum. The seal was carved from opal, contains iconography typical of ancient Phoenicia, and bears the inscription "belonging to Jezebel" (L'YZBL). The name Jezebel means "where is Baal?" and seems to have been reserved only for royalty.

The iconography and epigraphy match the 9th century BC, only about 1 percent of seals from this region and period belonged to women, and the name Jezebel in the time of ancient Israel is known only in association with the Phoenician princess of Sidon who married Ahab.

The infamous Jezebel was the daughter of Ethbaal, a 9th-century BC Phoenician king whose name appears to have been preserved in the Tyrian king list copied by Menander of Ephesus in the 2nd century BC. Jezebel met her fate at the royal palace of Jezreel, which excavations have revealed to be an ancient strategic fortress even larger than the royal citadel at Samaria. This fortress at Jezreel, which had a massive open courtyard, could have housed the significant chariot and cavalry force of Ahab. Jezreel was destroyed not long after the time of Jezebel and Ahab in the 9th century BC, probably by the Arameans, who had been involved in a series of battles with Israel for many years.

Even though the "Jezebel seal" was first published after being noticed on the antiquities market, analysis of the seal has also authenticated it as a genuine Phoenician artifact. Therefore, identification of the seal with Queen Jezebel of the northern kingdom of Israel in the 9th century BC is not only plausible, but the only viable option.

> *[Ahab] married Jezebel the daughter of Ethbaal king of the Sidonians*
> *(1 Kings 16:31).*

(49) THE IVORY HOUSE
(Samaria Ivories)

Date: 9th century BC

Discovered: Palace of Ahab, Samaria, Israel

Period: Divided Kingdom

Keywords: Ahab; palace; Samaria; ivory; Omri

Bible Passages: 1 Kings 22:39; Amos 3:15

While Omri originally constructed the palace at Samaria, his son and successor Ahab made additions, including what the book of Kings describes as "the ivory house." During excavations of the 9th-century BC Samaria palace of Omri and Ahab, a room or house north of the main palace section was discovered in which over 12,000 intricately carved ivory objects or fragments of objects were found, prompting the room to be associated with the ivory house of Ahab.[56] The many ivory pieces were used to decorate luxury furniture and perhaps also as independent pieces of artwork, filling the "house" or room with a theme of ivory décor.

However, the pieces were not merely geometric designs or plants, but also included images of animals and pagan iconography, such as the winged sphinx motif or depictions of gods and goddesses, which clearly violated the Mosaic Law and yet is consistent with the influence of Jezebel and the policies of Ahab.

Because of the iconography and due to similar ivory objects being found in Phoenicia, there is an apparent connection to the Phoenicians through Jezebel the wife of Ahab, but analysis of the ivories also revealed that letters used as fitting

---

[56] Amos, who functioned as a prophet in the early 8th century BC, soon after the reign of Ahab and before the fall of Samaria, mentioned the house of ivory, which was probably also a reference to the palace of Ahab.

marks on certain pieces were in the Hebrew script, demonstrating that Israelite artisans were involved in the construction of the furniture and possibly the ivory pieces themselves.

> *Now the rest of the acts of Ahab and all that he did and the house of ivory which he built and all the cities which he built, are they not written in the Book of the Chronicles of the Kings of Israel? (1 Kings 22:39).*

(50) King Jehu and the Assyrians
(Black Obelisk of Shalmaneser III)

Date: 825 BC

Discovered: Kalhu (Nimrud, Iraq)

Period: Divided Kingdom

Keywords: Jehu; Assyria; Shalmaneser III; Omri; tribute; Carmel

Bible Passages: 1 Kings 18:19-46; 2 Kings 9:1–10:36; 15:19-20; 2 Chronicles 22:7-9

In about 825 BC, near the end of his reign, Shalmaneser III of Assyria erected a commemorative obelisk[57] carved from black limestone in the city square of Kalhu near the White Obelisk of Ashurnasirpal I. Called the Black Obelisk of Shalmaneser III, this monument recounted 31 years of military campaigns and the foreign kings he subdued, using text and illustrations.

The cuneiform text not only mentions kings paying tribute, but panels on the obelisk depict five of those kings—Sua of Gilzanu (Iran), Jehu of the house of Omri, the king of Musri (Egypt), Marduk-apil-usur of Suhi (Mesopotamia), and Qalparunda of Patin (Turkey).[58]

On the second illustrative panel from the top, Shalmaneser III appears on the left, standing under a parasol with two Assyrian officials behind him, while king Jehu of Israel bows down with his face near the ground with two Assyrian officials also standing behind him.

---

[57] *Obelisk:* A tall monument with four sides and a tapering top, which was usually carved out of stone and contained writing and illustrations.

[58] This tribute of Jehu to Shalmaneser III occurred on Mount Carmel, which is near Jezreel, where Jehu assassinated Jehoram and Jezebel, and also the location where Elijah had defeated the prophets of Baal years before.

The following three panels around the obelisk depict Israelites bringing tributes of various gold and silver objects. Above the scene of Jehu is an Assyrian inscription that translates partially as "The tribute of Jehu, house of Omri. I received from him silver, gold..." The house of Omri refers to the royal Israelite dynasty of

kings founded by Omri, typically seen as the most powerful and famous monarch of the northern kingdom of Israel by foreign nations.

This is the earliest known image of an Israelite king, an independent source confirming Jehu as the king of Israel in the 9th century BC, and one of four inscriptions of Shalmaneser III that mention Jehu.[59] Jehu son of Nimshi, king of Israel, is recorded in Kings and Chronicles as eliminating the previous dynasty and taking the throne from Jehoram in the northern kingdom of Israel during the 9th century BC. The inscription on the obelisk refers to Jehu as part of the "house of Omri" in the sense of a successor in the line of northern Israelite kings, since Omri had been dead for many years before the rise of Jehu.

At this time, the Assyrian Empire was one of the major powers of the world, and therefore it is not surprising to see an Israelite king bringing tribute to the Assyrian king Shalmaneser III, who had defeated and subjugated many nations, including Israel and their king.[60]

Tributes paid to kings by subdued or less powerful foreign nations were common in the ancient world. In fact, there is another tribute to the Assyrians by Israel recorded not long after the time of Jehu, when Menahem was forced to give tribute to Tiglath-Pileser III.

The image and text demonstrate that Jehu was the king of Israel in the 9th century BC during the dominance of the Assyrian Empire, following Omri, Ahab, and Jehoram, just as Kings and Chronicles record.

> *Search out Jehu the son of Jehoshaphat the son of Nimshi, and go in and bid him arise from among his brothers, and bring him to an inner room. Then take the flask of oil and pour it on his head and say, "Thus says [Yahweh], 'I have anointed you king over Israel'" (2 Kings 9:2-3).*

---

[59] Inscriptions on the Black Obelisk of Shalmaneser III, the Calah Bulls, the Kurba'il Statue, and the Marble Slab all mention Jehu.

[60] It is possible that the prophet Hosea referred back to Shalmaneser III and the destruction he caused in an attack (Hosea 10:14).

(51) Religion and the Masses
(Khirbet el-Qom Inscription)

Date: 750 BC

Discovered: Khirbet el-Qom, Israel

Period: Divided Kingdom

Keywords: Makkedah; Yahweh; Asherah

Bible Passages: 1 Kings 15:13; 16:33; 2 Kings 13:6; 17:16; 18:4; 21:3-7; 2 Chronicles 15:16; Ezra 7:6

On part of a pillar in a burial cave near Khirbet el-Qom, tentatively identified as Makkedah in Judah, a Hebrew inscription of six lines above a carving of a downward pointing hand was discovered chiseled into the stone. Based on the form of the letters, this inscription from Tomb 2 dates to about 750 BC, during the time of the divided kingdoms of Israel and Judah and the reign of King Uzziah of Judah, before the Assyrians attacked and conquered the northern kingdom of Israel.

The inscription mentions that the author, Uriyahu (a name meaning "my light is Yahweh" and known from the Bible to be used from the 11th to 5th centuries BC), was blessed by Yahweh and states that "by his Asherah he has saved him." The hand symbol may have had a spiritual significance, perhaps as the "magic hand" connected to divinity worship according to parallels from religious iconography found in the Middle East and Carthage, or it may have been connected to the metaphorical phrase "hand of Yahweh," which was commonly used in ancient Israel and is found in several books of the Bible.

It has been argued that this inscription is evidence for worship of a goddess named Asherah, who certain scholars suggest was considered the wife or consort of Yahweh in ancient Israel and Judah. However, the ancient Hebrew inscriptions mentioning the Asherah combined with information found in passages from the Old Testament that refer to the Asherah make it clear that this was a wooden object, such as a pole or sacred tree, that at times was used as a representation of Yahweh and did not designate a divine wife or consort of Yahweh.

At the site of Kuntillet Ajrud in the northeastern Sinai peninsula, a similar 9th-century BC inscription was discovered on a piece of pottery, referring to "Yahweh and his Asherah." The use of a wooden pole or tree as an idol associated with Yahweh is documented in the books of Kings and Chronicles from the 9th through the 7th centuries BC as an object that kings such as Asa, Hezekiah, and Josiah cut down and burned.

These inscriptions confirm that during the Divided Kingdom period, the people of Israel and Judah were worshipping Yahweh, but many of them also adopted and integrated pagan religious practices into their beliefs.

He rebuilt the high places which Hezekiah his father had destroyed; and he erected altars for Baal and made an Asherah (2 Kings 21:3).

(52) The Latrine of Desecration
(Iron Age Toilet Seat)

Date: 8th century BC

Discovered: Jerusalem, Israel

Period: Divided Kingdom

Keywords: Hezekiah; toilet; latrine; Jehu; desecration; pagan; ritual

Bible Passages:
2 Kings 10:18-28; 18:1-4; 2 Chronicles 31:1-2

Late in the reign of King Jehu of Israel, around 820 BC, Jehu destroyed the worshippers and the temple of Baal, the chief god of the Canaanite pantheon. As a specific act of desecration, Jehu broke down the temple of Baal in Samaria and "made it a latrine." This temple of Baal in Samaria was probably adjacent to the palace complex built by Omri and Ahab.

Excavations of the Baal temple have not been undertaken, however, because the Roman period temple of Augustus was built over the likely location, and since it has been partially preserved over the centuries, the Augustus temple structure has been left intact.

Yet, a recent discovery at Lachish has uncovered evidence for the particular act of desecrating a pagan temple or shrine with a latrine during the kingdom period of Israel and Judah. At Lachish, a major ancient city in the kingdom of Judah, King Rehoboam had built a six-chambered gate and walls in the late 10th century BC, similar to those his father Solomon had built earlier. The fortifications, which were noted in the book of Chronicles and discovered in archaeological excavations at Lachish, continued to be repaired and used throughout the kingdom period. Inside the chambers of the gate, soldiers were stationed, merchants sold items, city elders judged, and a religious shrine was even set up. In one of the chambers, steps led up to a high place where an offering table and two horned altars were discovered.

This shrine at Lachish was in use during the 8th century BC until it was intentionally destroyed and desecrated during the reforms of King Hezekiah beginning around 715 BC, in which he had pagan altars, shrines, and idols destroyed. Artifacts discovered inside the shrine area included the "belonging to the king" stamp impressions on jar handles that date to the reign of Hezekiah, and another stamp impression with the text "belonging to Nahum, my servant" who was probably a royal official at Lachish.

When the order was carried out at Lachish, the reformers not only chipped the "illegal" horns off the altars, but a stone toilet seat was placed in the shrine, which was then sealed up and never again used. Tests on this toilet seat found no traces of fecal matter, demonstrating that it was a ritual toilet meant to convey a theological message and not one that had come from another structure or been used at another time.

The discovery of this latrine or toilet seat demonstrates the peculiar practice of ritual desecration of pagan temples and shrines by Israelite and Judean kings of the 9th and 8th centuries BC, recorded in the book of Kings, and adds further archaeological evidence to the spiritual reforms of Hezekiah found at several other ancient cities.[61]

> *They also broke down the sacred pillar of Baal and broke down the house of Baal, and made it a latrine to this day (2 Kings 10:27).*

---

[61] The toilet seat pictured was discovered in Jerusalem, but it is of the same type found in the desecrated shrine at Lachish.

(53) The Reforms of Hezekiah
(Beersheba Horned Altar)

Date: 8th century BC

Discovered: Beer Sheva, Israel

Period: Divided Kingdom

Keywords: altar; Hezekiah; Beersheba

Bible Passages: Exodus 20:24-26; 27:1-2; 30:1-6; Joshua 8:30-31; 2 Kings 18:1-22; 2 Chronicles 4:1; 31:1-2

According to the Law of Moses, altars were supposed to be made of uncut stones or earth, while only the main altar and incense altar at the tabernacle and subsequently the temple were supposed to have horns. However, due to the influence of the surrounding nations and their religious rituals, many of the Israelites imitated the form of pagan altars and violated the stipulations that God had specified for altar construction, including the usage of horns outside the tabernacle or temple, altars of cut stones, and even images on the altars.

When Hezekiah became king of Judah, he ordered reforms and a return to following the commands God had given in the Law. As a result, standing stones, Asherah poles, high places, and illegal altars were destroyed.

Archaeological evidence of the reforms of Hezekiah have been discovered at multiple sites, but one of the most illustrative examples was found during excavations at Beersheba in the south of the kingdom of Judah. A horned altar made of finely cut sandstone and featuring an engraved image of a twisting serpent was found broken, dismantled, and reused as building stones in an 8th-century BC wall of a storehouse from the time of Hezekiah.[62]

The broken remnants of the horned altar from Beersheba have been reconstructed, providing insight into practices and events of 8th-century BC Judah. Since cut stone altars and images were banned by the Mosaic Law, and horned altars were illegal outside of the designated tabernacle or temple administered by priests in Israelite worship practices, this dismantling of the altar at Beersheba seems to be connected to the religious reformation of King Hezekiah in which he commanded pagan altars, shrines, temples, and idols to be destroyed.[63]

> *All Israel who were present went out to the cities of Judah, broke the pillars in pieces, cut down the Asherim and pulled down the high places and the altars throughout all Judah and Benjamin, as well as in Ephraim and Manasseh, until they had destroyed them all (2 Chronicles 31:1).*

---

[62] The cut stone horned altar at Beersheba was about 62 inches (157 cm) tall, while the width is unknown but was at least 3 cubits on each of the 4 sides, or possibly 5 cubits. The serpent may connect to the "Nehushtan" (2 Kings 18:4). The storehouse in which the pieces of the altar had been reused was probably destroyed during the campaign of Sennacherib against the kingdom of Judah in about 701 BC.

[63] Other "illegal" horned or cut stone altars from the Divided Kingdom period have also been discovered at Dan, Dothan, Kedesh, Megiddo, Shiloh, Shechem, Gezer, Lachish, and Arad.

(54) ISAIAH THE PROPHET'S SEAL
(Bulla of Isaiah)

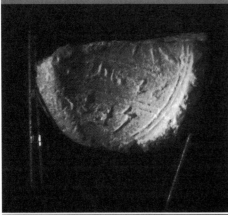

Date: 8th century BC

Discovered: Jerusalem

Period: Divided Kingdom

Keywords: Isaiah; prophet; Hezekiah; seal; bulla; Jerusalem

Bible Passages: 2 Kings 19:1-7; 1 Chronicles 1:29; Isaiah 1:1; 60:7; Hebrews 11:37

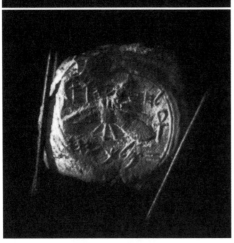

A clay bulla,[64] made from a stamped impression of a signet ring, was excavated in the Ophel area in Jerusalem and appears to refer to Isaiah. Discovered in an archaeological layer dating from the 8th to 7th century BC, the artifact was found in the same context as a bulla of King Hezekiah of Judah and 32 others, just outside a building dubbed the "royal bakery" where administrators of the kingdom could have discarded old letters and their clay seals. The bulla, only 1.3 cm in diameter, contains the name Isaiah and what seems to be the word *prophet* in the archaic Hebrew script used during much of the monarchy period.

Divided into three registers, the top contains an image or a symbol, probably

---

[64] *Bulla/bullae:* A lump of clay molded around a cord and stamped with a seal.

of an animal, while the middle and bottom lines contain text. Although partially broken, most of the letters are preserved, and it appears to read L-YSAYH[W] NBY[A] ("belonging to Isaiah, prophet"). The suggestion that the NBY[...] could be a name is unlikely, since there is only one previously known and rare personal or place name associated with those first three letters, Nebaioth, and there does not appear to be sufficient space for the W and T on the final line of the bulla.

If referring to the only attested prophet in Jerusalem from the 8th and 7th centuries BC named Isaiah, who was a respected spiritual advisor of King Hezekiah, this would be the first contemporary archaeological evidence yet discovered for Isaiah the prophet.

Isaiah, a prophet and son of Amoz, ministered during the reigns of kings Uzziah, Jotham, Ahaz, Hezekiah, and Manasseh, living from around 760–680 BC, prophesying from about 740–686 BC, and possibly executed in the reign of Manasseh.

> *In those days Hezekiah became mortally ill. And Isaiah the prophet the son of Amoz came to him (Isaiah 38:1).*

(55) THE TOMB
INSCRIPTION OF SHEBNA
(Shebna Lintel)

Date: 8th or 7th century BC

Discovered: Jerusalem

Period: Divided Kingdom

Keywords: Shebna; tomb; inscription; Jerusalem

Bible Passages: 2 Kings 18:18–19:2; Isaiah 22:15-23

A three-line Hebrew text dating to the 8th or 7th century BC was found inscribed into a limestone lintel above the entrance to a tomb in the Siloam area of Jerusalem.[65] The inscription refers to the entombed deceased who served as an official in the court around the time of Hezekiah of Judah.

Translation of the inscription shows that the tomb belonged to a man who held the title of royal steward ("who is over the house"). Although only the ending "yahu" portion of his name has been preserved, since a section of the inscription

---

[65] The lintel measures about 160 cm long and 52 cm tall. The form of the letters places the date of the inscription somewhere around 700 BC, and it is extremely similar to the Siloam Inscription.

was carved out in antiquity, the missing space would perfectly accommodate the word for "tomb" and the missing first four consonants in the name Shebnayahu. The text also warns possible looters that there is no silver or gold inside, but only the bones of the man and his handmaiden, and ends with a curse for any who would open the tomb.

According to analysis of the inscription, the location of the tomb, and comparison with the book of Isaiah, the tomb and inscription probably belonged to Shebna the royal steward of King Hezekiah of Judah around 700 BC.[66]

Isaiah recorded that in the period before Sennacherib attacked Jerusalem, Shebna was the steward "in charge of the royal household" and had a grand tomb made for himself that was carved out of rock and at a place of prominence overlooking the city of Jerusalem. But he eventually lost the title to Eliakim and seems to have been demoted to the position of royal scribe. Shebna probably had the tomb constructed in the late 8th century BC and might have been buried there in the 7th century BC.

> *Come, go to this steward,*
> *To Shebna, who is in charge of the royal household,*
> *"What right do you have here,*
> *And whom do you have here,*
> *That you have hewn a tomb for yourself here…?"*
> *(Isaiah 22:15-16).*

---

[66] A bulla dating from about 700 BC was recently found, impressed from a Hebrew seal reading "Shebnayahu, servant to the king," which would have belonged to the same Shebna the royal steward mentioned in Kings and Isaiah.

(56) Hezekiah and the Water Tunnel
(Siloam Inscription)

Date: 701 BC

Discovered: Jerusalem

Period: Divided Kingdom

Keywords: Siloam; tunnel; Hezekiah; Sennacherib; pool; inscription; Jerusalem

Bible Passages: 2 Kings 20:20; 2 Chronicles 32:1-4,30; Isaiah 22:9-11

The Siloam Inscription, a commemorative Hebrew text engraved onto the limestone wall of an underground tunnel beneath Jerusalem in about 701 BC, describes in brief the story of the cutting of a water tunnel by two teams of workers who started at the opposite ends of the tunnel—one group at the Gihon Spring and one group behind the city walls.

In 1880, a boy discovered the 6-line inscription inside the water tunnel and only about 19 feet from the opening to the Pool of Siloam or the Pool of Hezekiah.

However, the inscription was later cut out of the wall, removed, and eventually placed on display in Istanbul.

The text recounts how the stonecutters used axes to excavate through the rock along a natural fissure from both sides, eventually hearing a voice from the other side when there were only 3 cubits between them, finally meeting, and completing the tunnel of 1200 cubits from the water source to the pool underneath 100 cubits of rock. This tunnel, about 1750 feet long (533 m) and approximately 150 feet under the surface, connected the Gihon Spring with the Pool of Siloam.

With Jerusalem facing imminent attack from the Assyrians, King Hezekiah ordered the carving of the new tunnel just prior to the siege of Jerusalem by Sennacherib and his Assyrian army in 701 BC. The tunnel was masterfully engineered with a gradient of only 0.06 percent, allowing the water to flow slowly from the spring to the pool.

According to the Bible, the project was undertaken in order to provide a reliable and protected water source for the Judeans inside the walls of the city and to cut off the water supply from the Assyrian attackers outside of Jerusalem.

Although a few scholars have attempted to dispute the date and an association of the inscription with Hezekiah, analysis of the writing style, recent radiometric tests, and information from the ancient historical documents clearly place the date at the time of Hezekiah and Sennacherib.

The inscription and the tunnel in which it was found illuminate and corroborate the description of the construction project during the time of Hezekiah and the Assyrian siege of Jerusalem, recorded in the books of Kings, Chronicles, and Isaiah.

> *Now the rest of the acts of Hezekiah and all his might, and how he made the pool and the conduit and brought water into the city, are they not written in the Book of the Chronicles of the Kings of Judah? (2 Kings 20:20).*

(57) THE SIEGE OF LACHISH
(Lachish Reliefs)

Date: 700–681 BC

Discovered: Palace of Sennacherib (Nineveh, Assyria)

Period: Divided Kingdom

Keywords: Lachish; Sennacherib; Nineveh; Assyria; siege

Bible Passages: 2 Kings 18:7-17; 2 Chronicles 32:9; Isaiah 36:1-2

Several years after the northern kingdom of Israel fell to the Assyrians in ca. 722 BC, Hezekiah decided that the kingdom of Judah should not serve the Assyrians, and he ceased being a vassal of Assyria, paying tribute, and taking orders. As would be expected, this rebellion by Hezekiah prompted a forceful response by Sennacherib and the Assyrian army, and they launched a campaign around 701 BC to conquer and subdue Judah.

Using a brilliant military strategy, the Assyrian king Sennacherib began by conquering and destroying the fortified cities and towns of Judah before besieging the capital city of Jerusalem. The siege of Lachish was a strategic victory, and one in which the Assyrians apparently took great pride, since after the campaign Sennacherib had elaborate stone wall panels created to recount the battle through illustrations, and then installed them in room 36 of his South-West palace at Nineveh.

The panels, which specifically mention Lachish, were also compared to the site of Lachish, and analysis was able to demonstrate a match between the walls on the panels and the walls at the ruined city.[67] In exquisite detail, the reliefs covered the walls of a large room 39 feet (12 m) by 16.7 feet (5.10 m).

The panels show the Assyrian army and their siege engines, the soldiers of Judah attempting to defend their walled city of Lachish, the fall of the city, the torture and execution of men of Judah, the deportation of men, women, and children, and the enthroned Sennacherib revered in victory.

The reliefs are one of the great pieces of historical art from the ancient world, and not only tell the story visually, but show the armor and weaponry of soldiers, siege tactics, walls and towers of Lachish, and the extreme violence of the Assyrians. Archaeological excavations at Lachish corroborate that the Assyrians used a siege ramp, their prolific use of arrows, the fall of the city, and the brutality of the Assyrians. King Sennacherib commemorated this successful siege, and on one panel had himself portrayed enthroned as his victorious commander stood before him, while Judeans bowed down.[68]

Remains of the siege ramp that the Assyrians used to infiltrate the city were discovered, hundreds of Assyrian arrowheads were found, and bones of approximately 1,500 people—men, women, and children—including hundreds of skulls, were also discovered in mass burial in caves near the site. The campaign, including the conquest of Lachish, was also recorded in official Assyrian records and the books of Kings, Chronicles, and Isaiah.

Now in the fourteenth year of King Hezekiah, Sennacherib king of Assyria came up against all the fortified cities of Judah and seized them. And the king of Assyria sent Rabshakeh from Lachish to Jerusalem to King Hezekiah with a large army (Isaiah 36:1-2).

[67] An informative inscription on one of the panels reads: "Sennacherib, the mighty king, king of the country of Assyria, sitting on the throne of judgment, before [or at the entrance of] the city of Lakhisha [Lachish]. I give permission for its slaughter."

[68] It is thought that the panels had to be made to illustrate and commemorate the siege of Lachish rather than the capital city of Jerusalem, since the Assyrians failed to capture Jerusalem.

(58) SENNACHERIB VERSUS HEZEKIAH
(Sennacherib Prisms)

Date: 691 BC

Discovered: Palace of Sennacherib (Nineveh, Assyria)

Period: Divided Kingdom

Keywords: Sennacherib; Nineveh; Assyria; Hezekiah; Judah; campaign; prism

Bible Passages: 2 Kings 18:13–19:37; 2 Chronicles 32:9-21; Isaiah 36:1–37:38

The Annals of Sennacherib, recorded in about 691 BC, document eight campaigns, including one against the kingdom of Judah. The annals are currently known from three different cuneiform prisms—the Taylor Prism, the Oriental Institute Prism, and the Jerusalem Prism, plus eight additional fragments from other prisms that have not survived intact. As official records of the greatest accomplishments of the king, undoubtedly many copies were distributed throughout the empire.

The baked clay prisms that have been preserved and recovered are hexagonal, measuring about 38 centimeters tall and 14 centimeters across, and each of their six sides is covered in 500 lines of Assyrian cuneiform. These texts probably all originated in Nineveh, although the only reliable record of discovery location is for the Taylor Prism, which was found in the armory at Nineveh in about 1835.[69]

---

[69] The Oriental Institute Prism and the Jerusalem Prism were both discovered on the antiquities market, so their exact origin locations are unknown.

On column 3 of the prism, the text mentions the campaign of Sennacherib against the kingdom of Judah in 701 BC, the taking of 46 fortified cities, the deportation of 200,150 people and countless animals, the siege of Jerusalem, King Hezekiah, and the forced tribute payment to the Assyrians by Judah.

A portion of the translated text states: "As for Hezekiah, the Judean who did not submit to my yoke, I surrounded and conquered 46 of his strong-walled towns as well as the small towns in their area, which were without number, by leveling with battering rams and by bringing up siege engines, and by attacking and storming on foot, by mines, tunnels, and breeches, I besieged and took them. 200,150 people, great and small, male and female, horses, mules, asses, camels, cattle, and sheep without number, I brought away from them and counted as spoil. He himself I shut up in Jerusalem, his royal city, like a bird in a cage…Fear of my lordly splendor overwhelmed that Hezekiah. The warriors and select troops he had brought in to strengthen his royal city Jerusalem, did not fight…Hezekiah there felt the fear of the power of my arms, and he sent out to me the chiefs and the elders of Jerusalem with 30 talents of gold and 800 talents of silver…and all kinds of valuable treasures."

According to the book of Kings, Sennacherib demanded a tribute payment from Hezekiah of 30 talents of gold and 300 talents of silver, to which Hezekiah seems to have added 500 more, since the Assyrian records specify that Hezekiah gave Sennacherib 30 talents of gold and 800 talents of silver, plus other treasures, which was obviously over and above what had been the initial required payment.[70]

The Assyrian army encircled and laid siege to Jerusalem, attempting to force a surrender and absorb Judah into the Assyrian Empire, but the Assyrian records are silent after the siege and tribute and do not claim that Jerusalem was captured.

The Bible finishes the story, documenting that the Assyrians failed to take the city due to the death of their officers and mightiest warriors and returned to Nineveh in shame. Neglecting to mention the failure to capture Jerusalem and the death of many of the Assyrian soldiers in the royal annals of Sennacherib is to be expected based on the normal protocols of official records in the ancient Near East.[71]

The king of Assyria required of Hezekiah king of Judah three hundred talents of silver and thirty talents of gold. Hezekiah gave him all the silver which was found in the [temple of Yahweh], and in the treasuries of the king's house (2 Kings 18:14-15).

---

[70] The Bull inscription of Sennacherib housed in the British Museum also records information about this tribute of Hezekiah to Sennacherib.

[71] That Sennacherib was later assassinated and his throne usurped by his son Esarhaddon (2 Kings 19:37; Isaiah 37:38) suggests that his failure at Jerusalem had shown him to be weak and created an opening for a coup. The assassination of Sennacherib by his sons and the acquisition of the throne are also recorded in official Assyrian sources.

(59) THE FALL OF NINEVEH
(Nineveh Chronicle)

Date: 550 BC

Discovered: Southern Iraq (exact location unknown)

Period: Divided Kingdom

Keywords: Nineveh; Assyria; Babylonians; Nabopolassar;

Bible Passages: Isaiah 10:12; Jeremiah 50:17-18; Nahum 2:8-10; Zephaniah 2:13

The Nineveh Chronicle is a tablet that was composed in about 550 BC as part of a series of historical records assembled and preserved by the Babylonians. It is the main source of written historical information on the destruction of the city of Nineveh, which in turn led to the fall of the Neo-Assyrian Empire. Although other ancient texts preserve and record the events, this tablet is by far the oldest and originated from official government records of the war, recounting major events of the years 616–609 BC with 75 lines of cuneiform text.[72]

In 612 BC, a coalition led by the Babylonians under King Nabopolassar in his fourteenth year, with help primarily from the Medes, conquered and destroyed

---

[72] This tablet is 13.2 centimeters long and 6.9 centimeters wide, and was repaired from four fragments.

what was then the largest city in the world, the Assyrian capital of Nineveh, after a three-month siege. The chronicle notes that the army plundered the city and the temples and turned the city into a ruin heap.[73]

Archaeological evidence of this destruction includes razed buildings and the discovery of more than 40 skeletons in the ruins of the conquered city. The Assyrian king Sinsharishkun died, probably a suicide, but an Assyrian prince named Ashuruballit II escaped and continued a minor resistance until the battle of Carchemish in 605 BC, when the Neo-Assyrian Empire was finally eliminated, and the Babylonians reigned supreme.

The kingdom of Judah had been repeatedly attacked by the Assyrians, suffering defeats and tribute payments, but surviving. The prophets Nahum, Zephaniah, and Jeremiah mentioned the fall of Nineveh and the Assyrians, and no doubt many of the people saw divine justice carried out when Assyria was defeated. However, only a few years after Nineveh was destroyed, the Babylonians forced Judah into becoming a vassal state, eventually leading to a series of rebellions by Judah and the destruction of Jerusalem and the temple.

> *He will stretch out His hand against the north*
> *And destroy Assyria,*
> *And He will make Nineveh a desolation,*
> *Parched like the wilderness*
> *(Zephaniah 2:13).*

---

[73] A translated section of the tablet reads, "They encamped against Nineveh…for three months they subjected the city to a heavy siege…they inflicted a major defeat upon a great people. At that time Sinsharishkun, king of Assyria, died. They carried off the vast booty of the city and the temple and turned the city into a ruin heap" (Nineveh Chronicle, ABC 3).

(60) Arad and the Temple of Yahweh
(Arad Yahweh Ostracon)

Date: 7th century BC

Discovered: Arad, Israel

Period: Divided Kingdom

Keywords: Arad; ostracon; temple; Jerusalem; Yahweh; Eliashib

Bible Passages: 1 Kings 1:50; 2:28; 6:37; 2 Kings 25:9

Among over 180 ostraca discovered at Arad in southern Judah from various periods was a cache of 91 currently known Hebrew ostraca found in the citadel of Arad and dating to around 600 BC or earlier, before the time of the Babylonian destruction of the city.[74] Most of these Hebrew ostraca, written with black carbon ink on sherds of pottery, are letters about supplying the military at the fortress with wine, flour, and oil, or the movement of troops.[75]

Many of these letters were written to Eliashib son of Eshiyahu, who seems to have been the quartermaster or commander at the fortress of Arad.[76] The room in

---

[74] The Hebrew ostraca date from the 10th to 6th centuries BC, but the Eliashib ostraca are from a small window of time.

[75] Recently, multispectral imaging revealed more writing on the back of Ostracon 16 from this cache, demonstrating how more information could be recovered from ancient artifacts.

[76] Three bullae were also found at Arad impressed with the Hebrew phrase "belonging to Eliashib son of Ehiyahu."

which they were found, located in the south side of the fortress, was even designated the "house of Eliashib."

One of the letters to Eliashib mentions a cryptic command and mysterious matter, and the sender ends stating that everything is well because an unnamed man "is in the house of Yahweh."[77] This "house of Yahweh" was the phrase used for the temple of the Lord (Yahweh) in Jerusalem known from many books of the Bible. The context of the letter seems to indicate that this unknown man was seeking refuge in the temple and was now safe, perhaps going through the process of "grasping the horns of the altar" in the temple courtyard—an asylum ritual mentioned in the book of Kings.

Since this ostracon to Eliashib was written before the 587 BC destruction of Jerusalem and the temple by the Babylonians under Nebuchadnezzar II, the phrase "house of Yahweh" would be referring to the temple Solomon had originally built in Jerusalem, and it is possibly the oldest surviving artifact yet discovered that provides contemporary evidence for the temple of Yahweh in Jerusalem.[78]

> *The nineteenth year of King Nebuchadnezzar, king of Babylon, Nebuzaradan the captain of the guard, a servant of the king of Babylon, came to Jerusalem. He burned the house of [Yahweh], the king's house, and all the houses of Jerusalem (2 Kings 25:8-9).*

---

[77] This particular "House of Yahweh ostracon" artifact was designated Ostracon 18.

[78] The "Jehoash Inscription," if authentic, refers to the temple of Yahweh in Jerusalem and dates to the 9th century BC.

CHAPTER 6

EMPIRES OF BABYLON AND PERSIA
(Jeremiah–Malachi)

When books describing the Babylonian and Persian periods such as Daniel and Esther came under critical analysis, many scholars asserted that these were either full of historical errors or even in the genre of historical fiction. The most famous failed critique of the book of Daniel was the mystery of the king named Belshazzar, who was unknown in any other sources and considered a fabricated character until an official Babylonian document was discovered that specifically named Belshazzar. The book of Esther, which has often been considered a novel rather than a historical account, has also received valuable contributions from archaeological discoveries, including artifacts that mention names, architecture, and governmental organization specified in the text of Esther.

In 605 BC, during the reign of Jehoiakim of Judah, the famous Babylonian general and king Nebuchadnezzar II subdued the kingdom of Judah, made it a vassal of the Babylonian Empire, and began taking people into exile back to Babylon. The people of Judah resisted being dominated by Babylon, and a revolt led to a siege of Jerusalem that resulted in the destruction of the city and temple in 587 BC. Many more people were taken into exile to Babylon and the surrounding area, living under the rule of pagan kings such as Nebuchadnezzar and Belshazzar in an unfamiliar place.

But in 539 BC the Persian army captured Babylon, and Cyrus allowed the exiles to return home. A few returned to Jerusalem and rebuilt the temple, finishing it in 517 BC. Many, however, continued to live in various parts of the Persian Empire, such as Esther and Mordecai in Susa during the reign of Xerxes I. Years later, in 444 BC, Nehemiah was granted permission by Artaxerxes I to return to Jerusalem and led the people in rebuilding the walls of the city, persisting through opposition from local officials.

During the Persian period, the final books of the Old Testament were written, followed by the "four hundred years of silence" between Malachi and John the Baptizer. The artifacts from the Babylon and Persia section were discovered primarily at various locations in the lands that once comprised ancient Judah, Babylon, and Persia. Many of the artifacts are ancient texts and inscriptions of the Babylonians and Persians that record information about events also found in the Bible, contributing to our overall historical knowledge and demonstrating the accuracy of the biblical texts.

(61) BARUCH, SCRIBE OF JEREMIAH
(Bulla of Baruch)

Date: 600 BC

Discovered: Jerusalem, Israel

Period: Babylon and Persia

Keywords: Baruch; Jeremiah; scribe; Jerusalem

Bible Passages: Jeremiah 32:12; 36:1-32; 43:1-7; 45:1-5

Two clay seal impressions (bullae) reading "belonging to Baruchyahu son of Neriah the scribe" in ancient Hebrew script were discovered in Jerusalem and later appeared on the antiquities market. The first of these seal impressions was probably found inside what is known as the "Burnt House" that was destroyed during the Babylonian conquest of Jerusalem in 587 BC. The seal impressions, which specify the profession of Baruch and the name of his father, date to around 600 BC and the time of Jeremiah.[79] Since in approximately 600 BC Jeremiah had a scribe in Jerusalem named Baruch son of Neriah, the seal that formed the impressions seems to have belonged to this Baruch who wrote the words of Jeremiah the prophet.

Scrolls, such as the books Jeremiah dictated, would be sealed with the name

---

[79] Baruch and Baruchyahu are the same name, but the longer version has the Yahu (Yahweh) theophoric element attached. Other seals and clay stamp impressions of people mentioned in the book of Jeremiah have also been discovered, including "Jehucal son of Shelemiah" (Jeremiah 38:1), "Gedalyahu ben Pashur" (Jeremiah 38:1), and a seal of "Baalyisha king of the Ammon" (Jeremiah 40:14).

of the writer or owner, although Jeremiah may have had his own seal for his letters and prophetic works. However, the Baruch seal impressions demonstrate that Baruch son of Neriah was a historical person in Jerusalem during the time of Jeremiah the prophet, and that he was a scribe, as stated in the book of Jeremiah.

> *Then Jeremiah took another scroll and gave it to Baruch the son of Neriah, the scribe, and he wrote on it at the dictation of Jeremiah all the words of the book which Jehoiakim king of Judah had burned in the fire (Jeremiah 36:32).*

(62) LETTERS TO LACHISH
(The Lachish Ostraca)

Date: 600 BC

Discovered: Lachish, Israel

Period: Babylon and Persia

Keywords: Lachish; ostracon; Azekah; Jeremiah; Zedekiah; Nebuchadnezzar; Babylonians

Bible Passages: 2 Chronicles 36:11-21; Jeremiah 34:6-7; 37:5; 38:19; Habakkuk 1:1-6; Zephaniah 1:4-13

The Lachish Letters are a series of 21 recovered letters written in Hebrew, using black ink on sherds of pottery, found in the destroyed ruins of Lachish. The letters illuminate conditions and events in Judah just before the Babylonians under Nebuchadnezzar reconquered and destroyed Judah and Jerusalem in ca. 587 BC. This attack should not be confused with the earlier attack and destruction of Lachish by the Assyrians in about 701 BC.

The defeat at the hands of the Babylonians was predicted by Habakkuk and Zephaniah and recorded by Jeremiah, Kings, and Chronicles. Archaeological discoveries have demonstrated the destruction of major cities such as Lachish and Jerusalem, and ancient documents provide additional details that match the information recorded in the Bible.

Scholars disagree about where the letters were sent from, although at least some of them seem to have been sent from Jerusalem to Lachish. Most of the letters are written from Hoshayahu, a military officer who was in charge of an outpost near Lachish, to Yaush, the military commander at Lachish.

The Lachish Letters mention military commanders, armies, palace intrigue, and intelligence reports and record at least three major events involved in the war against

Babylon that are also described in the Bible—a conspiracy against Zedekiah by supporters of Babylon, a diplomatic mission to Egypt, and Lachish and Azekah being the last remaining unconquered cities before Jerusalem.

The letters also mention the "prophet" and the name Jeremiah. Letter 1 mentions a son of a man named Jeremiah, although the exact identity of this Jeremiah is unknown. Letter 2 mentions the military commander Yaush, and a blessing from Yahweh, and many of the letters make reference to Yahweh, demonstrating that even though the nation had fallen into apostasy, there was still a remaining belief in God. Letter 3 mentions a warning from the "prophet" and a mission to Egypt.[80] The success of this diplomatic mission to Egypt was reported in the book of Jeremiah.

Letter 4 notes that Lachish and Azekah were the last cities that were conquered before Jerusalem, which the book of Jeremiah also recorded.[81] Letter 6 describes a conspiracy against the king by the princes, who apparently want to side with the Babylonians. This event was also documented by Jeremiah, who was told by King Zedekiah about the Judeans who betrayed him and wanted to hand him over to the Babylonians.

Letter 7 might state the name of the prophet as Jeremiah, although the ink is faded so the reading is uncertain. However, since Jeremiah was the only prophet known in Judah at this time, and the name does appear in the letters, it is likely that the Lachish Letters refer directly to Jeremiah the prophet and attest his existence and involvement in affairs of the state that were recorded in Kings, Chronicles, and Jeremiah.

Then Jeremiah the prophet spoke all these words to Zedekiah king of Judah in Jerusalem when the army of the king of Babylon was fighting against Jerusalem and against all the remaining cities of Judah, that is, Lachish and Azekah (Jeremiah 34:6-7).

---

[80] "The servant Hoshaiah has sent to inform my lord Yaosh. May Yahweh cause my lord to hear news of peace…it has been reported to your servant saying, 'The commander of the army, Coniah son of Elnathan, has come down in order to go into Egypt and to Hodaviah, son of Ahijah, and his men he sent to me to obtain supplies from him,' and as for the letter of Tobiah, servant of the king [Zedekiah], which came to Shallum son of Jaddua through the prophet, saying, 'Beware,' your servant has sent it to my lord" (Letter #3).

[81] "We are watching for the signal stations of Lachish, according to all the signals you are giving, because we cannot see the signals of Azekah" (Letter #4).

(63) NEBO-SARSEKIM
THE CHIEF EUNUCH
(Nebo-Sarsekim Tablet)

Date: 595 BC

Discovered: Temple of Marduk (Sippar, Iraq)

Period: Babylon and Persia

Keywords: Nebo-Sarsekim; Jeremiah; Nebuchadnezzar; eunuch

Bible Passage: Jeremiah 39:1-3

The Babylonian "chief officer" Nebo-Sarsekim, mentioned in passing once in the book of Jeremiah, was an official in the service of Nebuchadnezzar II who was virtually unknown to history and had no particular influence on events recorded in the book of Jeremiah.

However, when a small cuneiform tablet only 2.13 inches (5.4 cm) long and 1.38 inches (3.5 cm) wide was found in storage at the British Museum and translated, suddenly this unknown character helped to make the case for the historical reliability of Jeremiah.

Excavated in the ancient Mesopotamian city of Sippar and originally from a temple dedicated to Marduk, the contents of the tablet were rather mundane, simply stating, "1.5 minas of gold, the property of Nabu-sharrussu-ukin [Nebo-Sarsekim], the chief eunuch, which he sent…to [the temple] Esangila…year ten Nebuchadnezzar, king of Babylon." The tablet dates to year ten of Nebuchadnezzar (ca. 595 BC), and the donor was Nebo-Sarsekim, the chief eunuch.

The tablet is of great historical significance, however, since Nebo-Sarsekim is also mentioned in the book of Jeremiah as being present with Nebuchadnezzar and his officials at the capture of Jerusalem in ca. 587 BC before the city was destroyed. According to Babylonian documents, the "chief eunuch" was one of the highest ranking officials in the Babylonian court, and there was only one man in this position. Therefore, this temple receipt confirmed the existence of Nebo-Sarsekim as the chief officer or eunuch under Nebuchadnezzar in about 595 BC, just eight years before he was seen by Jeremiah at the Middle Gate in Jerusalem, demonstrating the historical accuracy of a passage in Jeremiah.

All the officials of the king of Babylon came and sat in the Middle Gate—Nergal-Sharezer, Samgar, Nebo-Sarsekim the chief officer… (*Jeremiah 39:3 AUTHOR'S TRANSLATION*).

(64) The Babylonian Conquest of Judah
(The Jerusalem Chronicle)

Date: 6th century BC

Discovered: Unknown, Mesopotamia

Period: Babylon and Persia

Keywords: Jerusalem; Nebuchadnezzar; Jehoiachin; Zedekiah; Carchemish

Bible Passages: 2 Kings 24:8-18; 2 Chronicles 36:8-11; Jeremiah 24:1; 46:1-26; Ezekiel 17:12

A cuneiform tablet often abbreviated ABC 5 and known as the Nebuchadnezzar Chronicle or the Jerusalem Chronicle, part of the greater Babylonian Chronicles, records information covering the first 11 years of the reign of Nebuchadnezzar II from 605–594 BC, including his military campaigns against Assyria, Egypt, and Judah.

Although the exact location of its origin is unknown since it was acquired on the antiquities market, this clay tablet measuring about 3.25 inches (8.25 cm) long and 2.4 inches (6.19 cm) wide has been verified as a genuine official document of the Babylonian period.

The chronicle reports that Nebuchadnezzar II "crossed the river to go against the Egyptian army which lay in Carchemish. They fought with each other and the Egyptian army withdrew before him. He accomplished their defeat and beat them to nonexistence."

Pharaoh Necho II, who had previously taken King Jehoahaz captive and appointed Jehoiakim as king of Judah, was defeated by the Babylonians in the battle of Carchemish ca. 605 BC when the Assyrian Empire disintegrated, and Egypt received a blow it never recovered from. Jeremiah the prophet also wrote about the battle of Carchemish and the defeat of Egypt.

The Jerusalem Chronicle goes on to recount that in year seven of Nebuchadnezzar II, about 597 BC, Nebuchadnezzar attacked Jerusalem, captured Jehoiachin, and appointed Zedekiah king. It specifies that "the king of Babylonia called out his army and marched to Hattu. He set his camp against the city of Judah [Jerusalem] and on 2nd Adar he took the city and captured the king [Jehoiachin]. He appointed a king of his choosing [Zedekiah] there, took heavy tribute and returned to Babylon."

Jehoiachin, or Jeconiah, king of Judah, reigned only three months and ten days because the Babylonian army took him captive to Babylon and placed his uncle in power as a puppet king. The books of Kings, Chronicles, and Jeremiah also mention the 597 BC siege of Jerusalem by Nebuchadnezzar, capture of Jehoiachin, and appointing of Zedekiah, which were historical events corroborated by this independent Babylonian account from the 6th century BC.

> *At that time the servants of Nebuchadnezzar king of Babylon went up to Jerusalem…So he led Jehoiachin away into exile to Babylon…Then the king of Babylon made his uncle Mattaniah king in his place, and changed his name to Zedekiah (2 Kings 24:10,15,17).*

(65) Nebuchadnezzar and the Image
(Nabu Statue)

Date: 800 BC

Discovered: Temple of Nabu at Kalhu (Nimrud, Assyria)

Period: Babylon and Persia

Keywords: Nabu; Nebuchadnezzar; statue; idol; Daniel; Jonah

Bible Passages: Daniel 3:1-30; Jonah 3:3-10

A statue from Assyria that may represent the god of wisdom known as Nabu (or Nebo) was part of a pair of inscribed limestone statues found at the temple of Nabu in Kalhu, Assyria. Other than these, there are no other known ancient statues of Nabu still in existence.

The statue was carved around 800 BC in the reign of Adad-Nirari III, during whose time Jonah visited Nineveh. The inscription praises Nabu and thanks the god for his deliverance, ending with a command that the reader should not trust in another god.[82]

---

[82] It has also been suggested that this Nabu inscription relates to the repentance of the king of Nineveh, the Assyrians' temporary turn from violence, their deliverance from destruction, and a possible reflection of syncretizing the message that Jonah brought about God with the Assyrian god Nabu.

However, the statue also provides a rare illustration of an official idol from the period of the Assyrian and Babylonian Empires. King Nebuchadnezzar II, ruler of Babylon, set up a golden image for the people to worship that probably resembled this statue, albeit on a much larger scale and coated with gold. The massive statue Nebuchadnezzar erected may have been a monument to the god Nabu—the god whom Nebuchadnezzar invoked in his name. Alternatively, the golden image possibly represented Nebuchadnezzar himself, as it was not typical practice to display statues of gods outside of their temples.

King Nabonidus, who reigned about six years after Nebuchadnezzar died, preferred the Sumerian moon god Sin, and his Verse Account of Nabonidus from shortly after the time of Nebuchadnezzar describes a similar situation in which Nabonidus had a new image of the god Sin constructed and erected, demonstrating that the practice of constructing and erecting new statues of gods was carried out by kings of the Babylonian Empire.

The choice to refuse to bow down and worship the golden image was considered religious blasphemy in ancient Babylon and could result in execution by burning in a furnace or oven. When Shadrach, Meshach, and Abednego refused to serve the Babylonian gods and worship the image, their punishment was reflective of what is known from the 6th-century BC Babylonian Letter of Samsu-iluna, which commands that those who have committed blasphemy against the gods be thrown into the kiln to be burned and destroyed by intense flames.[83]

> *Nebuchadnezzar the king made an image of gold, the height of which was sixty cubits and its width six cubits; he set it up on the plain of Dura in the province of Babylon (Daniel 3:1).*

---

[83] The passage in Daniel indicates a lime kiln, which had an opening at the top in which to place the initial materials for melting, and the Babylonian word for the place of burning, translated as "oven" or "kiln," is the equivalent of the Aramaic word used for the furnace in the book of Daniel.

(66) EVIL-MERODACH IN PRISON
(Prayer Tablet of Amel-Marduk)

Date: 566 BC

Discovered: Borsippa, Iraq

Period: Babylon and Persia

Keywords: Evil-merodach; Amel-Marduk; Babylon; Nebuchadnezzar

Bible Passages: 2 Kings 25:10-30; Jeremiah 39:13; 52:31-34

Amel-Marduk, called Evil-merodach in many Bible translations, was the king of Babylon from ca. 562–560 BC, ascending to the throne after the death of his father Nebuchadnezzar II.

A cuneiform clay tablet, found in Borsippa in southern Mesopotamia, preserved a prayer of lament and appeal to the god Marduk, which Amel-Marduk (then named Nabu-shuma-ukin) had written while in prison.[84] Although it is unknown exactly why Amel-Marduk was imprisoned, the prayer text seems to indicate that he was the victim of a conspiracy by his enemies, who must have accused him of serious crimes against the king or the gods, since lesser offenses would probably have been overlooked due to his status as prince of Babylon.

Amel-Marduk was freed in about 566 BC, and when Nebuchadnezzar died, he became the new king and changed his name to honor Marduk. After becoming

---

[84] The clay tablet is 17.14 centimeters tall and 9.2 centimeters wide with cuneiform writing on both front and back.

king of Babylon, Amel-Marduk also released the former king Jehoiachin of Judah from prison, whom he had apparently met and become friends with when the two were both incarcerated during the reign of Nebuchadnezzar. After being imprisoned for 37 years and when he was about 63 years old, Jehoiachin was given a position of honor above the other exiled kings in Babylon.

The reign of Amel-Marduk was only two years, however, as he was murdered by his brother-in-law Neriglissar (Nergal-sar-ezer the Rab-mag), a former high official who had been present at the 587 BC destruction of Jerusalem. Neriglissar then usurped the throne and ruled ca. 562–556 BC during this tumultuous period of Babylonian history.

> *Evil-merodach king of Babylon, in the first year of his reign, showed favor to Jehoiachin king of Judah and brought him out of prison (Jeremiah 52:31).*

(67) JEHOIACHIN'S DAILY RATIONS
(The Ration Tablets)

Date: 6th century BC

Discovered: Babylon, Iraq

Period: Babylon and Persia

Keywords: Jehoiachin; Evil-merodach; Babylon; exile; ration

Bible Passages: 2 Kings 24:10-17; 25:27-30; Jeremiah 52:31-34; Ezekiel 1:2-3; 17:11-12

Jehoiachin, the king of Judah who had been defeated, taken in exile to Babylon, imprisoned, and then finally freed after 37 years, was also referred to in Babylonian records concerning daily rations. In a huge archive or library of official documents located in an underground vault near the Ishtar Gate in Babylon from the reign of Nebuchadnezzar and his son Amel-Marduk, dating to the period of approximately 595–560 BC, four ration tablets were discovered. The ration tablets in particular seem to have originated early in the reign of Amel-Marduk, beginning about 562 BC.

These cuneiform clay tablets were administrative documents that recorded the daily amount of oil allotted to Jehoiachin, the king of the land of Judah, five of his sons, and other captives. One of the tablets notes that ten sila of oil is distributed to the king of Judah, Yaukin (Jehoiachin, also called Jeconiah, is rendered as "Yaukin" in Babylonian documents), while two-and-a-half sila of oil is distributed to the sons of the king of Judah.[85]

---

[85] This tablet that mentions rations for Yaukin the king of Judah and the sons of the king of Judah is partially broken. The remaining tablet measures 9.2 centimeters tall and 10.5 centimeters wide. A sila was a Babylonian measurement equivalent to about 800 milliliters or 1.7 pints.

Another tablet about the sons of the king of Judah mentions rations for various craftsmen, and according to the book of Kings, among the captives taken at the time of Jehoiachin were the craftsmen and smiths.

The king who replaced Jehoiachin, his uncle Zedekiah, was hunted down after a rebellion, had his eyes gouged out, and his sons were executed for the same act of rebellion. The previous king, Jehoiakim, may have been executed in Babylon, but Jehoiachin fared much better than both his predecessor and successor, surviving and eventually being given a place of honor.

The book of Ezekiel also noted that Jehoiachin, king of Judah, was taken to Babylon with his family and continued to live there rather than being tortured or executed, as was the fate of many other defeated kings.

The Jehoiachin Ration Tablets, in specifying Jehoiachin as the king of Judah, that his sons were allowed to live, and that he was given daily rations in Babylon, which indicated greater status, and even continued to be referred to by his royal title confirm the accuracy of historical details recorded in the books of Kings, Jeremiah, and Ezekiel.

> *Jehoiachin changed his prison clothes and had his meals in the king's presence regularly all the days of his life; and for his allowance, a regular allowance was given him by the king, a portion for each day, all the days of his life (2 Kings 25:29-30).*

(68) BELSHAZZAR AND DANIEL
(Cylinder of Nabonidus)

Date: 550 BC

Discovered: Ur, Iraq

Period: Babylon and Persia

Keywords: Belshazzar; Nabonidus; Daniel; Babylon; Ur

Bible Passage: Daniel 5:1-31

The identity of Belshazzar, king of Babylon, had not been found in any sources outside of the book of Daniel until an ancient Babylonian text was discovered in 1854.

In about 550 BC, Nabonidus, king of Babylon, had placed four identical cylinders as foundation deposits at a temple in Ur of southern Mesopotamia. Recovered in excavations at the temple of the moon god Sin in Ur, this Cylinder of Nabonidus, king of Babylon, contains a 62-line cuneiform inscription in two columns.[86]

---

[86] The Cylinder of Nabonidus from Ur is 10.2 centimeters long and 5.1 centimeters in diameter, and contains two columns of 31 lines each.

Part of the text recorded an appeal to the moon god Sin and stated that "for me, Nabonidus, king of Babylon, save me from sinning against your great godhead and grant me as a present a life long of days, and as for Belshazzar my firstborn son, my own child, let the fear of your great divinity be in his heart, and may he commit no sin; may he enjoy happiness in life."

While the Nabonidus Cylinder from Ur primarily focuses on repairs made to a ziggurat for the moon god, the document also specifies that the eldest son of the Babylonian king Nabonidus was named Belshazzar.[87]

Another cuneiform text called the Verse Account of Nabonidus, found at Babylon, states that Nabonidus left Babylon on a long journey and entrusted the kingship to his firstborn son, whose identity as Belshazzar is known from the cylinders.[88] Nabonidus was the final Babylonian king until the Persians conquered Babylon in ca. 539 BC, and yet he had little interest in ruling from Babylon or managing typical affairs of the state.

Combining the evidence from these Babylonian documents illuminates the circumstances surrounding the reign of Nabonidus, including his departure from the capital and his appointment of his firstborn son, Belshazzar, as coregent to rule as king in Babylon. These documents not only confirm the existence of Belshazzar and his position as king of Babylon until the Persians captured the city, but the texts explain why Belshazzar would only be able to grant third place in the kingdom to anyone who interpreted the handwriting on the wall, since his father Nabonidus was first in the kingdom and Belshazzar was second.

These specific details about Belshazzar in the book of Daniel, confirmed by ancient Babylonian sources, demonstrate the exceptional accuracy of the book about political matters in Babylon during the 6th century BC that were forgotten in the following generations.

> *Then Belshazzar gave orders, and they clothed Daniel with purple... and issued a proclamation concerning him that he now had authority as the third ruler in the kingdom. That same night Belshazzar the Chaldean king was slain (Daniel 5:29-30).*

---

[87] A Cylinder of Nabonidus was also found at Sippar in southern Mesopotamia, but this contains a different text and should not be confused with the Ur cylinders of Nabonidus.

[88] The Nabonidus Chronicle states several times that King Nabonidus was not in Babylon, but the "prince" (Belshazzar) was there. The 5th-century BC Greek historian Xenophon, in *Cyropaedia*, wrote that the son of a Babylonian king, also called a king, was ruling in Babylon when the Persians conquered the city.

(69) THE PERSIANS CAPTURE BABYLON
(Nabonidus Chronicle)

Date: 4th century BC

Discovered: Babylon, Iraq

Period: Babylon and Persia

Keywords: Belshazzar; Nabonidus; Daniel; Babylon; Cyrus; Darius the Mede

Bible Passages: Daniel 5:25–6:2; 9:1-2; 11:1

The book of Daniel relates that Babylon was conquered, records that Belshazzar was slain, and then mentions Darius the Mede, rather than the Persian king Cyrus the Great, ruling the city of Babylon while no mention is made about a battle for the city.

A cuneiform document, recorded on a clay tablet and called the Nabonidus Chronicle, corroborates that there was no battle for the city and makes it clear that Cyrus was not leading the army at the capture of Babylon in 539 BC. Instead, a general from Media led the Persian army to Babylon and subsequently ruled the city as a governor.

The original text was probably written during the reign of Darius in the late 6th century BC, but the surviving copy seems to date to the 4th century BC or slightly later. The chronicle states that "the army of Cyrus entered Babylon without battle. Afterwards, Nabonidus was arrested in Babylon when he returned there...[later] Cyrus entered Babylon, green twigs were spread in front of him."

The identity of Darius the Mede mentioned in Daniel has been puzzling, but the Nabonidus Chronicle and related cuneiform documents may illuminate the situation, as the general from Media who led the army into Babylon also apparently served a short tenure of no more than four years in Babylon before dying.

Since cuneiform documents attest to another Persian official who ruled as the governor of Babylon from ca. 535–525 BC, perhaps Darius the Mede, who appears to have had a short rule and was already 62 years old when he took over Babylon, may have been the conquering general and initial governor of Babylon noted in the Nabonidus Chronicle.[89]

One of the most important texts of the time, the Cyrus Cylinder, affirms the capture of Babylon without a battle, stating that Cyrus was ordered "to march against his city Babylon…Without any battle, he made him enter his town Babylon, sparing Babylon any calamity."

An ancient Greek record, the *Cyropaedia* by Xenophon, agrees that the Persian army entered Babylon without a battle, but it also provides additional information that the Persians diverted the Euphrates to infiltrate the city and mentions that the acting king, who would have been Belshazzar, was killed after the Persians took the city.

Regardless of the identity of the mysterious Darius the Mede, multiple ancient documents agree with the narrative in the book of Daniel concerning the fall of Babylon to the Persians without a battle and the slaying of the king in Babylon.

> *That same night Belshazzar the Chaldean king was slain. So Darius the Mede received the kingdom at about the age of sixty-two (Daniel 5:30-31).*

---

[89] Ugbaru the Mede was the name of the conquering general and initial governor of Babylon according to the Nabonidus Chronicle, while Gubaru was the name of the official who subsequently ruled Babylon. Although unknown, it is hypothesized that "Darius" may have been a title or throne name for the governor ruling Babylon, and "the Mede" specified where he originated from and served to distinguish him from Darius the Persian, king of the empire. In ancient times, 62 years was beyond the normal life expectancy, and it would not be surprising if this official lived for only a few more years.

(70) RETURN FROM EXILE
(The Cyrus Cylinder)

Date: 539 BC

Discovered: Temple of Marduk (Babylon, Iraq)

Period: Babylon and Persia

Keywords: Cyrus; Babylon; Ezra

Bible Passages: 2 Chronicles 36:22-23; Ezra 1:1-4

Cyrus II, the Great, who ruled from ca. 559–529 BC, built one of the most expansive empires in the ancient world, combining ancient Media and Persia and conquering adjacent nations and assimilating them into what became the Achaemenid Persian Empire.

After the army of Cyrus captured Babylon in 539 BC, which is also an event inferred in the book of Daniel, Cyrus issued a decree that captive people could return to their homelands, restoring possession of their stolen sacred religious objects and destroyed temples. One of the original decree copies is preserved on the Cyrus Cylinder, which was rediscovered in Babylon where it had been placed as a foundation deposit in the Esagila temple of Marduk. Written to a Babylonian audience, it began by claiming that Nabonidus, the previous Babylonian king, had been a religious heretic and forced labor on the free people of the city, and so the gods had chosen Cyrus as a champion, liberator, and king of the world.

This Babylonian form of the decree addressed the god Marduk and stated, "Sanctuaries had been abandoned for a long time, I returned the images of the gods, who had resided there [in Babylon], to their places and I let them dwell in eternal abodes. I gathered all their inhabitants and returned to them their dwellings."

In the book of Ezra, the same decree of 539 BC was recorded, but it was written to Judah and referred to Yahweh rather than Marduk.[90] Cyrus sought to accommodate his different subjects and their religious views, which is why different deities were referred to depending on the specific audience. But since the Babylonians had looted and destroyed the temples of many nations, the general decree had the same essential results regardless of the culture it was addressed to.

The empire-wide decree found on the Cyrus Cylinder and the decree recorded in the book of Ezra are legally the same, but simply written to different people, and demonstrate the pluralistic policies of the Persians and the accuracy of the decree that Ezra recorded.

> *Now in the first year of Cyrus king of Persia [539 BC]... he sent a proclamation throughout all his kingdom, and also put it in writing... "[Yahweh], the God of heaven, has given me all the kingdoms of the earth and He has appointed me to build Him a house in Jerusalem, which is in Judah. Whoever there is among you of all His people, may his God be with him! Let him go up to Jerusalem which is in Judah and rebuild the house of [Yahweh]" (Ezra 1:1-3).*

---

[90] The Cyrus Cylinder presents Cyrus as a worshipper of Marduk, although ancient documents and research indicate that Cyrus was a religious pluralist who sought support throughout his empire by tolerating most beliefs so long as they did not cause problems for the government or lead to rebellion. There is no evidence that Cyrus worshipped the Ahura Mazda of Zoroastrianism, as the later Persian kings did, and essentially nothing is known of his personal beliefs.

(71) DARIUS, AHASUERUS, AND ARTAXERXES
(Achaemenid Royal Inscribed Bowl)

Date: 464 BC

Discovered: Hamadan, Iran

Period: Babylon and Persia

Keywords: Achaemenid; Persian; Darius; Xerxes; Ahasuerus; Artaxerxes; Esther; Nehemiah

Bible Passages: Nehemiah 1:1-3; 2:1-8; Esther 1:1–3:6

The Achaemenid Persian kings decorated their palaces with inscriptions of their lineage and achievements, images of themselves, and superb artwork. One exquisite gold fluted bowl contains an inscription in Persian, Elamite, and Babylonian that names and honors the king Darius the Great, while another set of four known silver bowls were inscribed naming the kings Artaxerxes I, son of Ahasuerus (Xerxes I), son of Darius the Great.

Numerous inscriptions of these kings have been found at both Susa and Persepolis. Darius was the king of Persia during events recounted in part of the book of Ezra, Ahasuerus was the Persian king who Esther married, and Artaxerxes was on the throne when Nehemiah served as cupbearer and governor.

During the time of Xerxes I (ca. 486–465 BC), which is the Greek rendering of Persian Xšayārša (Babylonian and Hebrew Ahasuerus), the king seemed to prefer his winter capital of Susa, where he planned and launched another campaign against the Greeks, hosted epic parties, and ruled over an empire stretching from India to Ethiopia.

According to Persian, Greek, and Hebrew sources, Xerxes returned home in 479 BC after the failed invasion, completed monumental construction projects in the capital cities of Persepolis and Susa, sought consolation in his harem, and selected a new queen.

Although Susa has been extensively damaged and pillaged both in antiquity and modern times, archaeological excavations at Susa have uncovered the citadel, the palace, the royal audience hall, the King's Gate, and numerous official inscriptions. Persian inscriptions at Susa state that Darius and Xerxes built and repaired the palace and the King's Gate. This monumental gate measured about 131 feet by 92 feet (34 m by 28 m) with a square central room of 69 feet (21 m) each side, supported by columns of at least 40 feet (12 m) in height.

The palace complex itself was situated in the northern part of Susa on a mound that occupied about five hectares. This complex, also referred to as the citadel, consisted of the palace where the king lived, the royal audience hall, and the monumental gate. Access to the palace complex was via a pavement of bricks that passed through a monumental passageway of two halls with double porticoes using a total of 72 columns and ended at the King's Gate. The royal audience hall, called the apadana, was built with massive columns that were decorated with capitals in the shape of bulls and lions.

Susa and its palace—including the royal hall, the King's Gate, and the "house of the women"—were the setting for events of the book of Esther, when she was selected to be the new queen of Xerxes in about 479 BC and held that position for at least six years.[91]

The Daiva Inscription of Xerxes (Ahasuerus) also lists the lands and people that are part of his empire, including India and Cush at the farthest reaches. Under the next king, Artaxerxes I, the cupbearer Nehemiah worked in the Susa palace and went before the king, probably in the royal audience hall, where Nehemiah requested that Artaxerxes allow him to return to Jerusalem and rebuild the city walls.

> Now it took place in the days of Ahasuerus...who reigned from India to [Cush] over 127 provinces, in those days as King Ahasuerus sat on his royal throne which was at the citadel in Susa, in the third year of his reign he gave a banquet for all his princes and attendants, the army officers of Persia and Media, the nobles and the princes of his provinces being in his presence (Esther 1:1-2).

---

[91] In addition to the kings themselves, a Persian cuneiform tablet from the end of the reign of Darius I or the beginning of the reign of Xerxes I, around 490 BC, mentions an official named Mordecai, or Marduka as the name was rendered in Babylonian. This tablet, found at Borsippa south of Babylon, names Marduka as a scribe and translator under the authority of Ushtannu, the satrap of the province of Babylon and Across the River, and may refer specifically to the Mordecai known from the book of Esther before he moved to the capital of Susa.

(72) Friends and Enemies of Nehemiah
(Elephantine Papyri)

Date: 5th century BC

Discovered: Elephantine, Egypt

Period: Babylon and Persia

Keywords: Elephantine; Passover; Sanballat; Hananiah; Bagoas; Johanan; Nehemiah

Bible Passages: 2 Kings 25:25-26; Nehemiah 2:10-19; 7:1-2; 10:16; 12:11-23; Jeremiah 41:17–44:1

The Elephantine Papyri, written in Aramaic during the period of about 495–399 BC and discovered on the island of Elephantine in southern Egypt, illuminate the life of a community of Judeans living during the Persian period, and mention a local temple of Yahweh, Passover observance, and several leaders. The ancestors of this group may have fled from Judah during the time of Jeremiah and the Babylonian conquests, eventually creating a settlement.

The "Passover Letter," from ca. 419 BC (Papyrus 6), contains reference to soldiers at the Judean garrison, then goes on to specify instructions for observing the Passover in the month of Nisan, demonstrating that some diaspora communities celebrated the festivals described in the Law of Moses from centuries prior. This letter was written by a military official named Hananiah who seems to have been in Jerusalem and can be tentatively identified with Hananiah, commander of the fortress mentioned by Nehemiah about 13 years before.

In another letter (Papyrus 30) from 407 BC, "Sanballat, governor of Samaria" and his sons are mentioned. Sanballat was one of three government officials who opposed Nehemiah and the rebuilding of the walls of Jerusalem in the 5th century BC. In this same letter, Bagohi, the governor of Judah, is addressed in regard to the rebuilding of the temple in Elephantine. Bagohi, or Bagoas, was governor of Judah after Nehemiah, but he is briefly mentioned in the book of Nehemiah prior to these events. Johanan the high priest in Jerusalem is also asked for permission in this letter, and according to Nehemiah, Johanan was the high priest there during part of the reign of Darius II (ca. 424–404 BC).

Therefore, not only do the Elephantine Papyri confirm the presence of a Judean diaspora community in Egypt mentioned in Kings and Jeremiah, but perhaps two governors, one military commander, and a high priest referenced in the book of Nehemiah are attested in the letters.

> When Sanballat heard that we were rebuilding the wall, he became furious and very angry and mocked the Jews. He spoke in the presence of his brothers and the wealthy men of Samaria and said, "What are these feeble Jews doing? Are they going to restore it for themselves?" (Nehemiah 4:1-2).

(73) GESHEM, KING OF QEDAR
(Bowl of Qaynu and Geshem)

Date: 430–410 BC

Discovered: Tell el-Maskhuta, Egypt

Period: Babylon and Persia

Keywords: Geshem; Qedar; Arabia; Nehemiah

Bible Passages: 1 Chronicles 1:29; Nehemiah 2:19; 6:1-2; Psalm 120:5

A cache of eight silver bowls from the time of the Persian Empire, including three with Aramaic inscriptions, were discovered in the area of Tell-el Maskhuta in eastern Egypt near the Suez Canal. Among the inscribed bowls was one dating to about 410 BC that mentions an offering to Han-'ilat by "Qaynu, son of Geshem, king of Qedar."

The people of Qedar (or Kedar) worshipped a goddess called Han-'ilat who was invoked in multiple Persian period inscriptions. Geshem, a king of Qedar, ruled from approximately 450–430 BC, while his son and successor Qaynu ruled from about 430–410 BC.[92] Although Geshem would have been based at their capital city of Adumattu in Arabia, his kingdom probably extended west to the Delta region of Egypt and north to the border of Judah.

The kingdom of Qedar was first mentioned by the Assyrians in the 9th century BC when they formed part of a coalition fighting against Shalmaneser III. Once Assyria fell, the kingdom of Qedar seems to have expanded substantially, reaching its peak around the 6th century BC.

---

[92] Another contemporary inscription mentioning Geshem of Qedar was discovered in Dedan, Arabia.

Nehemiah arrived in Jerusalem around 444 BC or soon after, which was during the reign of Geshem. During the time when Nehemiah was the governor of Yehud province in the Achaemenid Persian Empire, serving under Artaxerxes I in this position from approximately 444–432 BC, the nearby foreign leaders Sanballat, Tobiah, and Geshem the Arabian—who was king of Qedar—all opposed the rebuilding of the walls of Jerusalem. As a neighboring king, Geshem had interests and concerns about the bordering province of Judah, although the details of his reasoning for attempting to halt the rebuilding of Jerusalem and to assassinate Nehemiah are unknown. In spite of this opposition, Nehemiah was able to complete the project and Jerusalem was once again fortified.

> *Now when it was reported to Sanballat, Tobiah, to Geshem the Arab and to the rest of our enemies that I had rebuilt the wall, and that no breach remained in it… (Nehemiah 6:1).*

(74) Dead Sea Scrolls
(Great Isaiah Scroll)

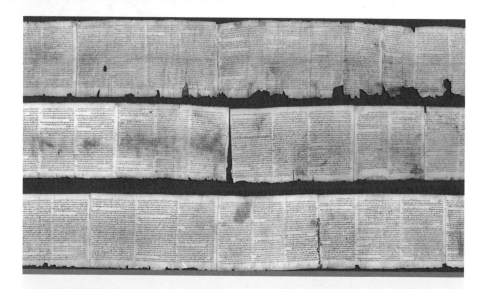

Date: 300 BC

Discovered: Cave 1, Qumran

Period: Intertestamental

Keywords: Dead Sea Scroll; Bible; Isaiah; scroll; Old Testament; Qumran

Bible Passages: Isaiah 1:1–66:24; 1 Peter 1:23-25

The Old Testament (Hebrew Bible) was written between about the 15th century BC and the 5th century BC, and almost completely in ancient Hebrew except for a few chapters, verses, and words. But until the 20th century, the oldest known Hebrew copies of the Old Testament were from the 10th century AD.

Then, in 1946, an incredible discovery was made when Bedouin shepherds came across ancient jars containing scrolls in a cave by the Dead Sea at Qumran.[93]

---

[93] The exact relationship between the Essenes who lived at Qumran and the scrolls is debated, but one theory is that the Essenes hid and preserved copies of the biblical scrolls when the Romans were coming to besiege Jerusalem in AD 70. The Essenes, discussed by the ancient writers Josephus, Philo, and Pliny the Elder, were a sect of Judaism that withdrew from society and lived in a devout religious community.

According to the commonly accepted version of the story, a shepherd boy was tending his flock of sheep when he threw a stone into a cave and heard something shatter. He investigated what was a broken jar in the cave and discovered that there were several jars with ancient scrolls inside.

Analysis of the scrolls found that many were Hebrew copies of books in the Old Testament, and it demonstrated their authenticity and antiquity. Subsequent archaeological excavations recovered more scrolls in the area.[94] These Hebrew scrolls, some of which date as early as around 300 BC, are extremely significant because they contain copies of the Hebrew Bible from 1,100 years or more before the Masoretic text, and yet demonstrate the accurate and reliable copying tradition of the Bible and the preservation of Scripture, as these scrolls are about 95 percent identical in most books with the much later Hebrew Masoretic text copies.[95]

The scroll of Isaiah, containing prophecies and historical records, was probably written over a period of many years, and possibly in two or three major sections, with the earliest known copy found among the Dead Sea Scrolls (1QIsaiah-a).[96] This particular Isaiah scroll has been assigned a date of around 300 BC.[97] Made from 17 pieces of parchment stitched together, this scroll is also noteworthy because it is a complete copy of the entire book, containing all 66 chapters except for a few small damaged areas.

The Dead Sea Scrolls make it clear that the Old Testament portion of the Bible was recognized as Scripture long before the time of Jesus since copies of these biblical books were found as a collection and referred to in commentaries among the various Dead Sea Scrolls.

The vision of Isaiah the son of Amoz concerning Judah and Jerusalem, which he saw during the reigns of Uzziah, Jotham, Ahaz and Hezekiah, kings of Judah (Isaiah 1:1).

---

[94] Currently, every book of the Old Testament has been found represented among the scrolls except for Esther. Esther may be discovered someday if more scrolls are recovered from the area, but it is also possible that the Essene community did not regard the book of Esther as Scripture due to the secular nature of the characters and therefore chose not to preserve it in their cache of manuscripts.

[95] In the few significant textual variations, the Dead Sea Scrolls often match the Septuagint rather than the Masoretic text, and certain passages in the Masoretic text seem to have been intentionally modified to match ideas and theology of medieval Judaism.

[96] The number *1* indicates Cave 1 at Qumran, and the letter *a* indicates that it was the first manuscript of Isaiah found in that particular cave.

[97] The Dead Sea Scrolls copy of Isaiah was dated by some C14 tests to around 350 BC, while a few scholars chose to argue that by paleography the manuscript was copied as late as ca. 150 BC.

CHAPTER 7

JESUS AND HIS WORLD

(Matthew–John)

Modern views about Jesus of Nazareth and the Gospels of Matthew, Mark, Luke, and John typically consider these narratives and the Jesus they describe to be based on a historical core, but also view them as a mythological construct formed and written in the generations subsequent to the life of Jesus by people who did not personally know Jesus and who were not eyewitnesses to the events.

Increasingly, however, archaeological data, and in particular many artifacts, demonstrate the accuracy and historical reliability of the Gospel narratives. In addition, the discovery of early manuscript copies of the Gospels imply the early composition of the accounts using eyewitness testimony.

After about 400 years of silence following the time of Nehemiah, during which Alexander the Great conquered much of the known world, Greek spread far and wide, the Roman Empire emerged, and the births of John the Baptizer and Jesus of Nazareth occurred.

Recorded in the Gospels of Matthew and Luke, the birth of Jesus took place when Augustus was emperor in Rome, Herod was the client king of Judea, and the temple in Jerusalem had been undergoing reconstruction. A census of the Empire had also just been ordered by Augustus, and then in 4 BC the prolific builder but paranoid king, Herod the Great, died, leaving his kingdom split between three of his sons and his sister. By AD 6, Judea had become a Roman province with a governor, and the Herodian family no longer ruled as kings.

Years later, during the ministry of Jesus, powers had shifted significantly as Tiberius now ruled the Empire, Pontius Pilate was the governor of Judea, Galilee was ruled by Herod Antipas, and Caiaphas was the acting high priest. Then, in AD 33, Jesus was crucified. Reports of His resurrection began to spread rapidly not only in Jerusalem, but around the entire region, and news of Jesus soon made its way to the Roman authorities.

The artifacts included in the section for the time of Jesus and the Gospels were discovered primarily in Judea and Galilee, with a high concentration in Jerusalem. The artifact types are varied and range from official stone inscriptions to coins to artwork to items that might otherwise seem commonplace or insignificant. All of the artifacts, however, illuminate narratives about the life of Jesus or demonstrate the historical accuracy of passages in the Gospels, or do both.

(75) HEROD THE GREAT AND THE TEMPLE
(Herodian Temple Donation Inscription)

Date: 20 BC

Discovered: Temple Mount, Jerusalem

Period: Jesus and the Gospels

Keywords: temple; Jesus; Jerusalem; Herod

Bible Passages: Luke 3:1-23; John 2:14-20

When Jerusalem and the temple were destroyed in AD 70, building fragments and artifacts were scattered around the side of the mount.[98] An inscription found in Jerusalem during excavations near the southern side of the ancient temple complex had originally been placed near the temple to commemorate the donation of an unknown amount of drachmas toward construction costs for a stone pavement, either for one of the courts of the temple or the outside courtyards of the complex.

This text also mentions the high priest, Simon son of Boethus, and the name of the donor, Paris son of Akeson from Rhodes. The Greek text, carved into limestone, refers to year 20 of the reign of Herod the Great, which was about 20 BC and also the year that temple reconstruction began under Herod.[99]

The first time that Jesus drove moneychangers and merchants from the temple courts, the Judeans said that the temple had been under construction for 46 years, which places that cleansing-the-temple episode in about AD 26. This also connects to the time of the beginning of the ministry of Jesus, just after the baptism of Jesus by John the Baptizer, which Luke records as occurring in the fifteenth year of the reign of Emperor Tiberius.

Although Tiberius became sole emperor in AD 14 after the death of Augustus, Tiberius actually received powers as emperor in AD 12, so counting to his fifteenth year from that point would also place the baptism of Jesus and the beginning of His ministry in about AD 26, in sync with the reference in the Gospel of John.

> *Then the Jewish leaders said to him, "This temple has been under construction for forty-six years" (John 2:20 NET).*

---

[98] A silver coin from ca. AD 134 also depicts the front of the Jerusalem temple that was destroyed in AD 70. The coin was overstruck on a Roman silver coin during the Bar Kokhba Revolt and reads "For the Freedom of Jerusalem" on the reverse. While the temple was destroyed about 64 years prior, at least a few people would have remembered seeing the grand and iconic structure early in their lifetime.

[99] A first-century AD ossuary or burial box, discovered in an ornate Roman period tomb outside ancient Jerusalem, was inscribed in Aramaic with "Simon, builder of the Temple" (*SMON BNA HKLH*). The ossuary, made of limestone, is of typical size, measuring 59 centimeters long, 28.5 centimeters wide, and 33 centimeters high. It has only the most basic decorations, but the two identical inscriptions were carefully made and easily read, unlike many ossuary inscriptions. The location of the tomb was immediately north of the walls of first-century AD Jerusalem. Financing the temple rebuild with tax money, King Herod the Great replaced every stone of the previous temple, employing 1,000 priests as masons and carpenters inside the actual sanctuary, while about 18,000 skilled laborers worked on the entire project. Thus, the Herodian temple was technically the third temple, but stood only until AD 70. Simon was one of those builders or skilled craftsmen, and his family honored him with a title commemorating his work.

(76) THE CENSUS OF QUIRINIUS
(Epitaph of Secundus)

Date: 1st century AD

Discovered: Beirut, Lebanon

Period: Jesus and the Gospels

Keywords: Quirinius; birth; Jesus; census; Syria

Bible Passages: Luke 2:1-3; 3:1; Acts 5:37

The successful and powerful Roman official Quirinius is found in only one sentence in the book of Luke, where he is named in connection to the census taken at the time of the birth of Jesus while serving as a ruler in Syria Province. Quirinius has also been found outside the book of Luke on an ancient tombstone epitaph of a Roman military officer, Quintus Aemilius Secundus, who served under the legate and former consul Quirinius in Syria.[100]

According to the epitaph, by order of the legate Quirinius, he conducted a census of the region of Apamene, Syria, totaling 117,000 citizens. Quirinius also ordered Secundus to fight the Ituraeans on Mount Lebanon, an area north of the Sea of Galilee that was part of the kingdom of Herod the Great. In addition to a census in Syria, the text mentions that Secundus was "in the service of the

---

[100] Secundus was memorialized by this 22-line Latin inscription after his death in the early 1st century AD. It was found in 1664 by Venetians in Beirut, which in Roman times was part of Syria Province. According to Tertullian, the Roman census around the birth of Jesus was taken by Saturninus, a governor or Legatus Augusti propraetor of Syria from about 9 to 6 BC. Quirinius may have been the Legatus Legionis in Syria Province, commanding at least three legions in the area at this time, which agrees with his portrayal as legate and military commander in the epitaph. The Deeds of the Divine Augustus is a first-century official biography of the emperor, and a valuable historical resource.

Divine Augustus," "under Publius Sulpi-
cius Quirinius the legate of Caesar in Syria,"
the Roman legion Legio I, and various titles,
allowing a probable date to be assigned for
the events and the creation of the epitaph.

Scholars have previously proposed con-
necting the inscription to a regional tax
assessment and acquisition of money from
the deposed Herod Archelaus in Syria
and Judaea, carried out by Quirinius and
Coponius, which Josephus recorded. However, the census in this inscription, which
was not a localized tax assessment, more
logically connects to the earlier Empire-
wide census ordered in about 8 BC and
documented in *Res Gestae Divi Augusti*, or
the Deeds of the Divine Augustus.

Almost the entirety of *Res Gestae* has been preserved from antiquity in monumental stone inscriptions discovered at Ancyra, Apollonia, and Pisidian Antioch.
A census of the whole Empire connected with Quirinius was stated by Luke as the
"first" census, while a second and later census was referred to in Acts. The Quintus Aemilius Secundus inscription reveals that the census was under the authority of the military, ordered by a legate and carried out by officers at the local level.

As a former consul in 12 BC, Quirinius was certainly deserving of the designation of "ruler, leader, or commander" of Syria stated in Luke. Further, since it
was Roman protocol for the military to conduct and oversee the census, it is logical that Luke would associate Quirinius the military commander with the census.
Therefore, the census mentioned in this inscription was conducted by Quirinius
around 8 BC or so as part of the census of the Empire that Augustus commanded,
and Luke recorded in relation to the birth of Jesus.

> *A decree went out from Caesar Augustus that a census be taken of all of
> the empire. This was the first census taken while Quirinius was a ruler
> of Syria (Luke 2:1-2 AUTHOR'S TRANSLATION).*

(77) COINS OF THE GOSPELS
(1st Century Coinage)

Date: 1st century BC and 1st century AD

Discovered: Judea and Galilee

Period: Jesus and the Gospels

Keywords: Herod; Archelaus; Antipas; lepton; mite

Bible Passages: Matthew 1:18–2:8; 2:22-23; 14:1-2; Mark 12:41-44; Luke 3:1

During the time of the Gospels and the 1st century, coins circulated throughout the Roman Empire, including in Judea and Galilee, in various denominations or values. These coins, usually made of bronze and silver but occasionally minted using gold, were issued by the emperor and by local rulers.

Typically, the coins displayed images associated with religious iconography or an image of a ruler, with inscriptions naming or honoring those rulers and occasionally the year of issue. These types of coins help to give precise dates to events within the Gospel narratives and confirm the existence and titles of several officials who lived at the time of Jesus, such as the Herodian rulers.

Herod the Great was designated as king of Judea by the Roman Senate in 40 BC, then sent back with an army, defeating both the Parthians and their allies the Hasmoneans. By 37 BC, Herod was in full control of the region with his capital at Jerusalem, and he had the support of Rome. Issuing his own coins as king, including one that depicted the cap and star of the Dioscuri, Herod utilized divine imagery found in Roman religion that also may have had meaning in Judaism connected with the star of a prophesied future ruler.

Throughout his reign, Herod demonstrated paranoia, opportunism, and violence, executing at least seven members of his family and numerous political rivals. By the time Jesus was born in Bethlehem, Herod was late in his reign and extremely fearful of losing power to a son or a usurper. Then, magi from the east came to his court asking about the recently born king of the Judeans whose "star" they had seen. The scribes told Herod the Great about a prophecy from the book of Micah that the ruler would be born in Bethlehem, and they may have also been aware of the prophecy about a star and ruler mentioned in the book of Numbers. To assure no rival would rise, Herod ordered the "Massacre of the Innocents," and word began to circulate about the birth of Jesus.

Herod Archelaus was a son of Herod the Great who inherited the largest part of the kingdom, ruling from 4 BC–AD 6 alongside his brothers Antipas and Philip and his aunt Salome. As the main heir, Archelaus received Judea and the title *ethnarch*, meaning ruler over a common ethnic group. He issued coins during his reign, including the bronze prutah with the name "Herod" surrounding grapes on one side and the title "ethnarch" with a helmet on the other side. He was such a brutal and pompous ruler that the Romans exiled him to Gaul in AD 6, then made Judea a province of the Empire. Because of Archelaus, Joseph avoided Judea and returned to Galilee after leaving Egypt, ruled by the much more reasonable Antipas.

Herod Antipas the tetrarch was a son of Herod the Great who ruled the Galilee area from 4 BC–AD 39 when Emperor Caligula banished him to Gaul. The coins of Herod Antipas often included Greek inscriptions mentioning his name and title "Herod Tetrarch" on one side and "Tiberias" in honor of the emperor on the other. Many of his coins depicted wreaths, palm branches, or reeds, and therefore were not pagan in their iconography.

The lepton was a tiny bronze coin and smallest denomination of Judean coinage originally minted in the early first century BC by the Hasmonean ruler Alexander Jannaeus. Two lepta coins equaled one quadrans, which was the lowest denomination of all Roman coins and amounted to only about one sixty-fourth of the daily wage for an agricultural worker. The buying power of a lepton was miniscule, as it would take eight to buy only one small sparrow.

Because of the durability of metal coinage, the lepton and many other coins originally minted in the Hasmonean period stayed in circulation through the 1st century AD and the time of the New Testament. The lepton was decorated on the obverse of the coin with an anchor and a Greek inscription mentioning "King Alexander," while the reverse depicts an eight-pointed star. While the lepton or half prutah of Alexander Jannaeus is the most known and most common, King Herod also issued lepton coins reading "King Herod" and having plant, animal, cornucopia, and anchor symbols.

The tiny lepton coin eventually came to be called a widow's mite because of the giving attitude of a widow who donated all the money she had, two of these small mites, to the temple treasury.

> *Now in the fifteenth year of the reign of Tiberius Caesar, when Pontius Pilate was governor of Judea, and Herod was tetrarch of Galilee... (Luke 3:1).*

(78) The Cana Wedding Jars
(Ritual Stone Vessels)

Date: AD 70

Discovered: House of Katros, Jerusalem

Period: Jesus and the Gospels

Keywords: purification; jar; Cana; water

Bible Passages: Mark 7:3-4; John 2:1-11; cf. Leviticus 11:36; 15:13

Stone vessels, carved out of the local soft limestone and often expertly crafted, were prolific in and around Judea Province and Galilee during the Roman period because of their common use in ritual purification for followers of Judaism. Beginning with the purity laws in the book of Leviticus about which materials became ritually impure and the use of "living water" to make them become clean, this idea had eventually been developed into a custom using water in stone vessels for purification. The primary purpose of this ceremonial washing was to become ritually rather than physically clean.

The craftsmanship of the vessels varies, being made both by hand or on a lathe, and the finished product ranges from crude and uneven to perfectly uniform with incised decoration. Some have even been discovered with inscriptions, such as personal names or chants.

At the Cana wedding in the Gospel of John, Jesus performed His first recorded miracle by turning water into wine inside large stone water pots typically used for purification rituals. The Gospel of John records that the six stone water jars contained two or three measures each, suggesting that the six were of slightly varying size.

Evidence indicates that there was an industry centered at Jerusalem for producing stone vessels, where the priests, festivals, and temple necessitated more frequent use. However, many stone vessels have been discovered all over the regions of Judea and Galilee from the 1st century BC and 1st century AD, and the large stone water jars have specifically been discovered in places such as Jerusalem and Cana. Yet, their general absence from Samaria and the predominantly Hellenistic and Roman areas of the region and their decrease in AD 70 and near disappearance after AD 135 further demonstrate their association with ritual in Judaism.

These large jars were usually about 26 to 32 inches high and 16 to 20 inches in diameter, agreeing with the size variance stated by John of two to three *metretas*, which was about 9 gallons (34 liters).

> *There were six stone water vessels set there for the Jewish custom of purification, containing two or three metretas each (John 2:6 AUTHOR'S TRANSLATION).*

(79) Moses Seat
(Magdala Stone Moses Seat)

Date: 1st century AD

Discovered: Magdala, Galilee

Period: Jesus and the Gospels

Keywords: Magdala; synagogue; Chorazin

Bible Passages: Matthew 23:1-12; cf. Nehemiah 8:4

On the west coast of the Sea of Galilee, the town of Magdala was one of several fishing and fish-processing centers located around the lake during the 1st century AD.[101] Discoveries at the town included commercial buildings located by the port, weights for fishing nets, a mosaic depicting a Galilean fishing boat, pools used for the processing of fish, a fountain house, and a 1st-century synagogue.

The synagogue is located near the main entrance to the city, and although it is one of several known 1st-century synagogues in Judea and Galilee, its state of preservation is exceptional. The main room of this synagogue is surrounded by stepped benches, a colorful mosaic floor on the periphery, and remnants of fresco painted walls. A second room, perhaps used as a study room, is adjacent to the meeting room.

---

[101] Matthew mentions that Jesus took the boat to the boundary of Magdala, perhaps indicating the boundary of the town (Matthew 15:39). Although a few early manuscripts copied the place name as "Magadan," no evidence exists for this name in ancient Galilee. In Mark, the parallel passage states that Jesus took the boat into the district of Dalmanutha (Mark 8:10), which is otherwise unknown but may have been a regional name for the area that Magdala was located in, or Dalmanutha might be a Greek transliteration of the Syriac word for harbor. Mary Magdalene was probably from this town (Luke 8:2).

Inside the main room of the synagogue, excavations uncovered an intricately carved stone, nearly cubed shaped, decorated with a menorah, ritual water jars, pillars, palm trees, and various geometric and floral designs.[102] The carvings might represent aspects of the temple in Jerusalem and provide a religious link between the synagogue and the temple.

The overall shape of the stone also resembles what is often called the "Moses Seat" known from a few other sites, including one from the synagogue at nearby Chorazin to the north.[103] Although there are differences of opinion, these stone "seats" seem to have been used as a place or table for the scrolls of the Hebrew Bible, with the books of Moses as foundational and thus the origin of the term.[104] Jesus mentioned the scribes and Pharisees placing themselves "in the chair of Moses," implying that they attempted to equate their authority and teaching with the books of Moses, a major section of the Bible.

The scribes and the Pharisees have seated themselves upon the Moses seat (Matthew 23:2 AUTHOR'S TRANSLATION).

---

[102] The measurements of the Magdala "Moses Seat" stone are 50 centimeters by 60 centimeters by 50 centimeters.

[103] An Aramaic inscription on the front of the "Moses Seat" from Chorazin honors Yudan son of Ishmael for making the colonnade and its staircase and suggests that as his reward he should have a share with the righteous. The Chorazin synagogue also has what appears to be a depiction of a Gorgon from Greek mythology carved into the stone as an architectural decoration.

[104] Other objects identified as a "Moses Seat" include those found in ancient synagogues at Hammath by Tiberias, Chorazin, En-Gedi, and possibly Delos.

(80) Caiaphas the High Priest
(Caiaphas Ossuary)

Date: 1st century AD

Discovered: Caiaphas family tomb, Jerusalem

Period: Jesus and the Gospels

Keywords: Caiaphas; priest; ossuary; Jerusalem; tomb

Bible Passages: Matthew 26:3-68; Luke 3:1-2; John 18:12-28; Acts 4:5-6

Joseph Caiaphas was the acting high priest in Jerusalem from about AD 18 to 36 according to information from the Gospels, Acts, Josephus, and perhaps the Mishnah. Josephus relates that Caiaphas was appointed by the Roman prefect Valerius Gratus and continued his tenure through the time of Pontius Pilate.

A recently discovered ossuary[105] of Miriam, the daughter of Caiaphas, excavated west of Jerusalem in the Elah Valley, contains an inscription demonstrating that the Caiaphas family was of the priestly lineage of Ma'aziah, a priest from the tribe of Levi who was appointed during the time of David.[106] However, the high priest Caiaphas himself is known from another ossuary recovered from a

---

[105] *Ossuary:* A box, usually carved from stone, which stored human bones and was placed in a tomb.

[106] It seems that the descendants of Ma'aziah, who were one of 24 families that served in the Jerusalem temple during ancient times, continued to be part of the priesthood for centuries (1 Chronicles 24:18; Nehemiah 10:8). The ossuary from the Elah Valley was produced between about AD 70–135, and its Aramaic inscription translates as "Miriam daughter of Yeshua son of Caiaphas, priest of Maaziah from Beth Imri."

1st-century AD tomb outside of ancient Jerusalem. Twelve ossuaries were found inside the tomb, two of which have the family name "Caiaphas" inscribed on them. One particularly ornate ossuary, carved from limestone, had a 1st-century AD Aramaic inscription reading *Yehosef bar Qayafa* ("Joseph, son of Caiaphas"), which fits the New Testament Greek spelling of the family name *Kaiafa* perfectly.

Skeletal remains of six different individuals were discovered inside the ossuary, including a man about 60 years old, which may be the bones of the high priest Caiaphas. The name, location, and decorative quality of the ossuary indicate that it was a burial box used for a wealthy and prominent Jerusalem citizen with the family name Caiaphas. Additionally, the date of the Caiaphas burial is before AD 70, when ossuaries ceased to appear in Jerusalem, but from AD 43 or later, indicated by an AD 43 coin of Herod Agrippa I found in the skull of one of the skeletons.

Since Caiaphas served as high priest until he was replaced in AD 36 with Jonathan son of Ananus, this chronology fits the time frame for when this high priest likely died. As the high priest, a Sadducee, and part of the Sanhedrin, Caiaphas was instrumental in the plot to kill Jesus by claiming charges of blasphemy and treason that would lead to execution. Ultimately, this led to the trial of Jesus before Caiaphas, who then sent him to the prefect Pontinus Pilate due to requirements of Roman law about capital punishment.

Those who had seized Jesus led Him away to Caiaphas, the high priest, where the scribes and the elders were gathered together (Matthew 26:57).

(81) PONTIUS PILATE THE GOVERNOR
(The Pilate Stone)

Date: AD 26–36

Discovered: Caesarea, Israel

Period: Jesus and the Gospels

Keywords: Pilate; governor; Tiberius; Caesarea

Bible Passages: Matthew 27:1-26;
John 19:1-15

Pontius Pilatus (Pilate) was appointed fifth prefect of Judaea Province in AD 26 while Tiberius was emperor. Pilate had an irregularly long term as prefect, governing for over ten years and having his tenure exceeded only by one other prefect, procurator, or legate of Judea (his predecessor, Valerius Gratus, ruled for a few months longer).

During this time, Sejanus, commander of the Praetorian Guard, had accumulated so much power and influence that he effectively ruled the Empire. Because Sejanus rose to power just before Pilate was sent to Judaea, Pilate may have been appointed by Sejanus rather than Tiberius, and this had political ramifications for Pilate relating to the trial of Jesus.

During his time as prefect, Pilate experienced at least six significant conflicts with the local population, with the last resulting in recall from the province in AD 36. One of these conflicts was the trial of Jesus. Since the Roman prefect had power over life and death, his approval was ultimately needed to sanction an execution.

After a series of events put Pilate at odds with many of the Judeans, matters were made more complicated when Sejanus was accused of a plot in AD 31 and subsequently executed without trial, followed by the arrest and execution of many of his associates.

The trial of Jesus in AD 33 came after Pilate had already angered the Judeans, and with a likely Sejanus association, he was in a delicate position that required him to stay in favor with the emperor. When the Judeans told Pilate if he released Jesus he was no "friend of Caesar," he would have clearly understood it as a threat to destroy his favor with Tiberius and endanger not only his career but his life. As a result, Pilate acted in his best interests and submitted to the pressure of the religious leaders.

While Josephus and Philo depict Pilate as cruel and strong, rather than aloof and accommodating as portrayed in the trial narratives of the Gospels, this change in attitude is understandable in light of the historical context and particular situation of Pilate.

Now, two artifacts are known that are directly connected to Pontius Pilate as prefect of Judea. In a staircase near the theatre at Caesarea Maritima, excavations discovered a monument stone reused as building material that had a dedicatory Latin inscription reading "Tiberium, Pontius Pilatus, Prefect of Judaea…dedicated." The inscription, dating between AD 26–36, refers to this Roman politician with his name, his title, and a dedication to the reigning Emperor Tiberius.[107]

More recently, a copper-alloy Roman-type ring bearing the name "Pilato" (Pilatus) was analyzed and the findings published even though it had been discovered in excavations about 50 years ago at the palace fortress site of Herodium near Bethlehem. It was finally cleaned and details of the inscription on the ring were seen for the first time. The oval-seal section of the ring is slightly less than one centimeter at its longest point, has an amphora design in the center, and is circled by six Greek letters that spell *PILATO* (equivalent to Pilatus in Latin).[108] The letters are inscribed so that they would be read left to right, but in a semicircle, on a surface that the ring would stamp.

Although Latin was used for most official Roman documents and inscriptions, in many of the provinces Greek was commonly used, and it is significant that the coins minted by Pontius Pilate in Judea also used Greek. The ring was discovered in a 1st-century AD archaeological layer from AD 71 or before, in a room with other 1st-century AD artifacts and coins of the First Judean Revolt against Rome.

Because the cognomen of Pilatus is of Italian origin and is unknown from any other person in ancient Judea, this ring almost certainly refers to Pontius Pilate

---

[107] The praenomen (personal name) of Pilate is unknown, but his nomen (family name) of Pontius suggests that his family came from Samnium in southern Italy, and his cognomen (additional name used to distinguish within a family) of Pilatus appears to be derived from a word for javelin and related to the military.

[108] *Pilato* is also the Greek form of the name used in the New Testament.

the prefect and would have been used during his tenure in Judea, but it may have been used by a lower-ranking Roman official performing tasks in the name of the governor rather than by Pilate himself. Prior to the discovery of this ring and the official inscription at Caesarea, Pilate was known only from manuscript copies of Josephus, Philo, Tacitus, the Gospels, Acts, and 1 Timothy.

> *They bound Him, and led Him away and delivered Him to Pilate the governor (Matthew 27:2).*

(82) CRUCIFIXION IN JUDEA
(Crucified Man Remains)

Date: 1st century AD

Discovered: Givat Ha Mivtar, Jerusalem

Period: Jesus and the Gospels

Keywords: crucifixion; Jehohanan; Jesus; Jerusalem

Bible Passages: Luke 24:36-40; John 19:15-42; 20:20-29

Various forms of crucifixion had been used as punishment by ancient cultures, but the Romans developed it into a science and an effective political tool. In the Empire, punishment by crucifixion was a public spectacle usually reserved for slaves, criminals of low standing, and rebels.

The Romans typically used a vertical pole with a beam across the top (patibulum), like a Latin T, or a vertical pole with an intersecting crossbeam, which according to early iconography and use of the titulus (sign with the name and title of the accused) placed above the head, was the type used for the crucifixion of Jesus.

The convicted would first undergo flogging with a flagellum or rods, sometimes placed in a furca (forklike yoke), or endure other forms of torture that severely weakened and could even kill them before they were placed on the cross. They then were bound to and forced to carry their crossbeam to the place of execution, if possible. After arriving, they would be nailed to the crossbeam and the stake. Nails, rather than ropes, were the standard means of attachment for crucifixion known from ancient records. These crucifixions were usually conducted outside of the sacred border of a city and along major roads so that all could see.

Skeletal remains of two individuals have been recovered that show conclusive signs of the use of nails in crucifixion during the 1st century AD in Judaea, indicating the men had been attached to the cross by placing nails in the wrists and feet. An iron nail about 4.5 inches long (11.5 cm) with remnants of wood was still present in the heel bone of one victim, a man identified as "Jehohanan the son of Hagkol" by the Aramaic inscription on the ossuary that contained his remains. In a more recently discovered example, a nail was found lodged between the bones of the wrist in another crucifixion victim from Judea.[109]

The severe trauma of preliminary beatings and nailing to the cross was extreme, and death was a result of hypovolemic shock (blood or fluid loss), heart failure, dehydration, asphyxiation, or stabbing by the soldiers. Survival was not an option for the crucified, but an excruciating and humiliating death that one hoped would be swift.

On Nisan 14 in AD 33, Jesus was sentenced to and endured death by crucifixion, experiencing the punishments, protocols, and sequences known from Roman sources and archaeology.

> *"See My hands and My feet, that it is I Myself; touch Me and see, for a spirit does not have flesh and bones as you see that I have." And when He had said this, He showed them His hands and His feet (Luke 24:39-40).*

---

[109] The specifics of Roman crucifixion practices, which relate to the way in which Jesus suffered and died as recorded in the Gospels, are detailed in Roman sources and ancient artwork. "You will soon go out the gate in that direction led with hands spread out on the patibulum which you will have" (Plautus, *Miles Gloriosus*). "They are bound to the patibula. They are bound and led around and fixed to the cross" (Clodius, *History*). "Still others extend arms on the patibulum" (Seneca, *Dialogue*). The Alexamenos Graffito (see next chapter) shows a mockery of Jesus on the cross with outstretched arms on the crossbeam.

Simon of Cyrene was forced to carry the crossbeam for Jesus (Matthew 27:32; Mark 15:21; Luke 23:26), and Jesus told Peter that in the future, when he was an old man, his hands would be stretched out, probably in reference to the crucifixion of Peter in AD 64 (John 21:18).

Jesus had His wrists, which are a component of the arm included in the Greek word translated "hands," nailed to the crossbeam (Justin Martyr, *Letter to Antoninus Pius*; Luke 24:36-40; John 20:20-29).

(83) JESUS ARTWORK IN ROME
(The Alexamenos Graffito)

Date: AD 90–200

Discovered: Palatine Hill, Rome

Period: Jesus and the Gospels

Keywords: crucifixion; Jesus; cross; Christian; Rome

Bible Passages: 1 Corinthians 1:22-24; Galatians 5:11

In addition to the accurate and detailed portrayal of Roman crucifixion in the Gospel accounts, the crucifixion of Jesus is also briefly described by a few Roman period writers and depicted on a wall in Rome.

In the late 1st century AD, while writing as an official Roman historian, Josephus recorded that Pilate had condemned Jesus to be crucified. Lucian, a Roman living in the 2nd century AD who enjoyed mocking Christians, thought that it was humorous how Christians worshipped a man who had been crucified. Celsus, another 2nd-century AD Roman who criticized Christianity, affirmed that Jesus was nailed to a cross. Around the same time, Justin, a pagan turned Christian, wrote to Emperor Antoninus Pius in defense of Christianity, mentioning the crucifixion of Jesus and how the events in the Gospels can be confirmed by checking the Roman records such as the Acts of Pilate.

The earliest known pictorial representation of the crucifixion of Jesus comes from Rome, found scratched into the plaster of a wall of the Paedagogium on the Palatine Hill. Known as the Alexamenos Graffito, the drawing shows Jesus on the cross with the head of a donkey, while a man standing on the ground looks up to the crucifixion victim with a raised arm. Below, an accompanying Greek inscription reads "Alexamenos worships (his) god." The drawing and text exhibits through mockery how the Roman pagan mindset viewed the crucifixion of Jesus as foolishness, as that worldview could not imagine how a god could be subjected to a painful and dishonorable execution reserved for criminals who were not Roman citizens.

Because the building it was found in association with was originally constructed ca. AD 90, then modified and partly buried ca. AD 200, the drawing and inscription date to somewhere within this period, demonstrating knowledge of Christianity and the crucifixion of Jesus in Rome as early as the end of the 1st century AD.

Not only do the accounts of the crucifixion of Jesus in the Gospels match what is known about Roman period crucifixion from various ancient sources and archaeological discoveries, but the event of Jesus being crucified in Jerusalem is confirmed by multiple sources in the 1st and 2nd centuries AD.

> *We preach Christ crucified, to Jews a stumbling block and to Gentiles foolishness (1 Corinthians 1:23).*

(84) THE TOMB OF JESUS
(Burial Bench in the Holy Sepulchre)

Date: 4th century AD

Discovered: Church of Holy Sepulchre, Jerusalem

Period: Jesus and the Gospels

Keywords: Jesus; tomb; burial; resurrection; church

Bible Passages: Matthew 27:57–28:7; Mark 15:42–16:8; Luke 23:50–24:12; John 19:38–20:7

Burial practices common in Judea during the Roman period involved preparing the corpse for burial by washing and anointing with oils, then wrapping it in a linen shroud before being placed in the tomb, as soon as possible after death.

Because easily cut limestone was available throughout the region, people utilized tombs carved into rocky hillsides or shafts into the ground, cut with chisels. Most of these tombs had an entryway that could be closed and opened by moving the rolling stone or blocking stone, a central chamber, and multiple extension chambers or burial benches. The tradition of ancestral tombs goes all the way back to early civilization and is embodied in the phrases "gathered to his people" or "gathered to his father."

The tomb of Jesus, however, was a new tomb in which no one had been interred, and which no one used afterward. Recent restoration work to the edicule surrounding the tomb of Jesus has confirmed that it was a single chamber tomb carved into a limestone hill during the 1st century.[110] Further, a stone bench consistent with an arcosolium tomb from the Roman period was protected underneath the current structure, the tomb was originally sealed with a large circular stone, and the Romans had built a temple over the site prior to the building of the church.[111]

This information accords with what was recorded in the Gospels and writings of the early church about the burial and the tomb of Jesus. Christians in Jerusalem then passed down a continuous memory of the location of the tomb from the time of the burial and resurrection in AD 33 until construction of the Church of the Holy Sepulchre was started in about AD 326.

According to the Gospels, the tomb of Jesus was a new tomb just outside the city walls, hewn out of rock, single chambered, having a bench on which to place the body, and sealed with a large stone. Due to the significance of the resurrection in Christianity, the tomb of Jesus has been remembered, revered, and preserved for almost 2,000 years.

> *[Joseph of Arimathea] went to Pilate and asked for the body of Jesus. And he took it down and wrapped it in a linen cloth, and laid Him in a tomb cut into the rock, where no one had ever lain (Luke 23:52-53).*

---

[110] The edicule in the Church of the Holy Sepulchre is a small structure or chapel that was built around the remains of the tomb of Jesus.

[111] An arcosolium tomb in the Roman period had a section carved out of the rock where the body of the deceased was placed, usually in the form of an arched recess and a flat stone bench.

(85) RUMORS OF THE RESURRECTION
(The Nazareth Inscription)

Date: AD 41-54

Discovered: Unknown, Judea or Galilee

Period: Jesus and the Gospels

Keywords: Jesus; resurrection; tomb; disciples; Claudius

Bible Passage: Matthew 28:11-15

In 1878, a stone slab with a 22-line Greek inscription that was an "Edict of Caesar" surfaced in Nazareth and was purchased by a French antiquities collector. Because the stone was acquired through the antiquities market, its exact place of discovery is unknown, but it has been affirmed as authentic and seems to have been issued in Judea Province or Galilee.

The language and the historical context of the beginning of the reign of Claudius indicates that the edict was made about AD 41 when Claudius became emperor of Rome.[112] The text specifically prohibits the moving or stealing of bodies

---

[112] Claudius is specifically mentioned by Luke as an emperor in power during the time of the establishment of the church (Acts 11:27-28).

from stone-sealed tombs with "wicked intent," compares it to an offence against the gods, and imposes an extreme new penalty of death for the crime. It states that if anyone has "extracted those who have been buried, or has moved with wicked intent those who have been buried to other places…or has moved sepulcher-sealing stones…You are absolutely not to allow anyone to move those who have been entombed…" Consequently, the edict describes the same type of tomb, a stone-carved tomb sealed with a large stone, which Jesus was buried in according to Judean custom, while Romans were typically cremated.

According to Matthew, the false story that the disciples stole the body of Jesus was spread by the religious leaders of Judaism via the Roman soldiers, and this rumor apparently reached the ears of the emperor. Therefore, the edict recorded on the Nazareth Inscription was probably a reaction to stories about the resurrection of Jesus Christ, and in particular the version that the Roman soldiers guarding the tomb were paid to say that the disciples of Jesus stole His body while they were asleep.

By the time of Claudius, knowledge of Christianity and the story of the resurrection of Jesus had spread throughout many areas of the Roman Empire, beginning to cause problems in the realms of religion, politics, and society, and Claudius seems to have attempted to prevent any future claims of the resurrection of the dead.

> "You are to say, 'His disciples came by night and stole Him away while we were asleep'"…And they took the money and did as they had been instructed; and this story was widely spread among the Jews, and is to this day (Matthew 28:13-15).

CHAPTER 8

THE FIRST CHRISTIANS AND THE EARLY CHURCH

(Acts–Revelation)

For a time, many scholars considered Acts and the epistles to be merely theological writings with little value as historical documents. Yet when excavations and intensive research were conducted, mounds of archaeological evidence began to surface that demonstrated Luke, the author of Acts, to be a flawless historian verified by many ancient artifacts. The epistles also have been shown to contain accurate historical statements and reflect their geographic and cultural contexts with precision.

Immediately following the crucifixion, burial, and resurrection of Jesus in AD 33, the book of Acts continues with the earliest gatherings of Christians and the beginning of the church. Encompassing the period of about AD 33–62, Acts presents a chronological historical narrative of the early church, while the epistles, which fall in the period of around AD 45–95, contain a few additional historical details and offer minor contextual information from the 1st century AD.

During the time in which the events in Acts occurred and the epistles were written, notable Roman emperors such as Tiberius, Claudius, Nero, Titus, and Domitian were in power, and all of these rulers performed actions that had significant effects on the early Christians.

The apostle Paul, whose conversion occurred on the road to Damascus in about AD 35, began his first missionary journey in about AD 45 or so, and continued in ministry until his execution in AD 67, while Peter was crucified in AD 64 during the Christian persecution initiated by Nero following the Great Fire of Rome. Around 30 years later, John, the last surviving apostle, was banished to Patmos by Domitian, where he wrote the book of Revelation.

Christianity had been firmly established and spread throughout the Roman Empire by this time, and the faith would continue to grow and influence, eventually being declared legal by the Edict of Milan in AD 313.

The artifacts for the Acts and epistles period were discovered all over the Roman Empire, and are reflective of the spread of Christianity and the missionary travels of the apostles. Many of the artifacts are official inscriptions that contain important names and historical information, while a few artifacts are statues, altars, artwork, an ossuary, and even an ancient New Testament manuscript. These artifacts substantiate much of the historical information recorded in the book of Acts and a few of the epistles, and illuminate the context of early Christianity in the time of the New Testament.

(86) Aretas the King and Paul
(Burial Inscription of Itaybel)

Date: AD 37

Discovered: Madaba, Jordan

Period: Apostles and the Early Church

Keywords: Paul; Aretas; Damascus; Nabatea

Bible Passages: Acts 9:19-25; 2 Corinthians 11:32-33

King Aretas IV Philopatris, or Haritat, came to power as king of Nabatea after the assassination of Obodas III, and enjoyed a long reign from 9 BC to AD 40. The Roman emperor Augustus recognized Aretas IV as a client king of the Empire, and the kingdom status for Nabatea lasted until Trajan transformed the region into the province of Arabia Petraea in AD 106.

Originally named Aeneas, Aretas was selected as his throne name, and official inscriptions usually read "Aretas, King of the Nabataeans, Friend of his People." His daughter, Phasaelis, originally married Herod Antipas the Tetrarch, but in about AD 26 when Herod Antipas divorced her and married Herodias, Phasaelis fled to her father Aretas IV. Not only did this divorce and remarriage face bold criticism from John the Baptizer, but combined with a previous border dispute it prompted Aretas IV to launch a military campaign against Herod Antipas. With a much larger force and treacherous assistance from Philip the Tetrarch, Aretas IV destroyed the army of Herod Antipas and took part of his lands.

The city of Damascus, which had been designated as part of the Decapolis region but fell under Herodian influence, seems to have been part of the territory gained by Aretas IV as a result of his victory. A few years later, around AD 35, the apostle Paul began preaching in Damascus after his conversion, which caused an uproar in the city. A plot was made to catch and murder Paul, and the governor under King Aretas IV was collaborating, guarding Damascus and planning to seize Paul. However, the Christians in Damascus helped Paul evade arrest and death by lowering him down the outside of the wall at night in a basket.

A Nabatean funerary inscription found near Madaba, south of Damascus, dates to AD 37, only two years after Paul narrowly escaped death in Damascus. The inscription mentions this Nabatean king Aretas IV and two of his governors, a father named Itaybel and his son, although a different governor probably ruled the Damascus area when Paul was pursued.

> *In Damascus, the governor under King Aretas was guarding the city of Damascus in order to arrest me (2 Corinthians 11:32 NET).*

(87) SERGIUS PAULUS ON CYPRUS
(Paulus the Proconsul Inscription)

Date: 1st century AD

Discovered: Soloi, Cyprus

Period: Apostles and the Early Church

Keywords: Sergius Paulus; proconsul; governor; Cyprus; Paphos

Bible Passage: Acts 13:4-14

Sergius Paulus was a Roman politician in the 1st century AD, serving under Emperor Claudius (AD 41–54), and is known to have held the offices of proconsul of Cyprus and curator of the banks and channel of the Tiber River in Rome.

A Roman period monumental stone with a dedication inscription written in Greek, discovered at Soloi in Cyprus, located north of the ancient capital city of Paphos, mentions the governor Paulus who served in the position of proconsul during part of the reign of Emperor Claudius. The inscription suffered damage in antiquity, but the majority of eight lines are still preserved.

Erected in honor of the father of Apollonius in the thirteenth year of Claudius, a portion of the text translates as "he also altered the senate by means of assessors during the time of the proconsul Paulus." Although the text mentions only the Paulus portion of his name, it does specify him as the proconsul or governor.

It is linguistically significant that Luke, the author of Acts, uses the Greek term *anthupatos* to designate the position of Sergius Paulus as proconsul. This Greek term is the equivalent of the Latin term proconsul. In about 22 BC, Caesar Augustus made Cyprus a senatorial province, which meant a proconsul would be ruling there rather than a prefect. Paphos had been made the Roman capital of the province, so the proconsul resided there at the praetorium, but his influence extended all around the island.[113]

While an exact date range for the time of this governor is not stated, the chronological context of the inscription places his tenure prior to about AD 53. Because Paul and Barnabas met the proconsul Sergius Paulus in Paphos around AD 45–46, this inscription from Soloi almost undoubtedly refers to that same governor who became a Christian during their missionary journey to Cyprus.[114]

When they had gone through the whole island [of Cyprus] as far as Paphos, they found a magician, a Jewish false prophet whose name was Bar-Jesus, who was with the proconsul, Sergius Paulus (Acts 13:6-7).

---

[113] Pliny the Elder, a 1st-century Roman author, noted that there were magi on the island of Cyprus, just as Luke recorded in the case of Elymas the magi (Acts 13:6-8).

[114] Sergius Paulus may also be referenced on a Latin inscription found at Pisidian Antioch. This inscription mentions L. Sergius Paulus, which is also the form of the name found in the context of the Tiber River curator in Rome. According to Roman history and archaeological sources, the Sergii family was prominent in the region of Pisidian Antioch, based at a large estate northeast of the city in Vetissus, but the family was originally from Italy. This L. Sergius Paulus was probably the proconsul and curator who Paul and Barnabas met at Paphos.

(88) LYSTRA AND DERBE DISCOVERED
(Lystra and Derbe Inscriptions)

Date: 2nd century AD

Discovered: Lystra and Derbe, Turkey

Period: Apostles and the Early Church

Keywords: Galatia; Lystra; Derbe; Timothy

Bible Passages: Acts 14:5-22; 2 Timothy 3:10-11

Lystra was a city in Galatia Province, located along the Via Sebaste in the Lycaonia region, southwest of Iconium, west of Derbe, and just north of the modern village of Hatunsaray. Lystra has not yet been excavated, but archaeological surveys of the site, Roman coins of colonia Lystra, and a stone altar from the 2nd century AD inscribed in Latin and bearing the name Lystra have allowed its identification.

The acropolis occupied about 16 acres, while below was probably the rest of the town built on the flat area and near the stream. Lystra was established by Augustus as a colony along the Via Sebaste, and an inscription on a statue from Pisidian Antioch, donated by the colony of Lystra, also demonstrates this designation. The locals revered Zeus, and a temple dedicated to him outside the city walls has been tentatively identified by scanning technology. Hermes, often regarded as the messenger of Zeus, was another prominent god in the area.[115]

---

[115] Ovid, who was familiar with the region, wrote a story taking place nearby in which the gods Zeus and Hermes appeared in human form and went to 1,000 homes in the area seeking hospitality. Only the elderly couple Philemon and Baucis were hospitable to them, and for this they were spared from wrath by flood, which destroyed the valley and its people. Forty years later in Lystra, the hometown of Timothy, Paul, and Barnabas proclaimed the gospel and

For many years, the precise location of Derbe in Galatia Province was unknown. Besides references in Acts, the city was mentioned in Roman period texts such as the writings of Cicero and Strabo, but nothing had been discovered that allowed definite identification of the site. Eventually, however, inscriptions and coins were found that pinpointed the site at Kerti Hüyük in Lycaonia about 80 miles (130 km) southeast of Lystra and demonstrated that it was occupied in the Roman period by people who spoke Latin and Greek.

Discoveries include a dedication inscription honoring Emperor Antonius Pius by the town council and the citizens of Derbe in the 2nd century AD, another inscription about Michael the bishop of Derbe from the Byzantine period, and Roman coins that state both the name of the city, Derbe, and the region, Lycaonia.

In about AD 47, Paul and Barnabas left Lystra for Derbe after Jews from Pisidian Antioch and Iconium attempted to assassinate Paul and left him for dead. According to Acts, many disciples were made in Derbe on the first visit, and Derbe was the only city in Galatia where Acts and the epistles did not record persecution. Gaius of Derbe, probably a Roman citizen, is mentioned accompanying Paul, Timothy, and others on later missionary travels, and inscriptions in the area from the Byzantine period demonstrate that Christianity had taken root at Derbe in antiquity.

> *They became aware of it and fled to the cities of Lycaonia, Lystra and Derbe (Acts 14:6).*

Paul miraculously healed a lame man in about AD 47, but the locals mistook Paul for Hermes and Barnabas for Zeus, syncretizing Christianity with polytheism.

(89) THE CITY AUTHORITIES OF THESSALONICA
(Politarch Inscription)

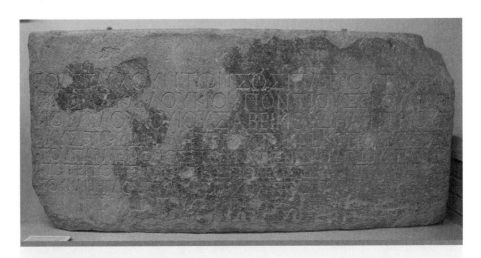

Date: AD 155

Discovered: Thessalonica, Greece

Period: Apostles and the Early Church

Keywords: Thessalonica; politarch; Greece; Macedonia

Bible Passages: Acts 17:1-9; 19:29; 27:1-2

The city of Thessalonica in Macedonia, named after princess Thessalonike, came under Roman control in 168 BC but was made a free city. During the Roman period, Thessalonica was ruled by local officials with the Greek title *politarch* (meaning "city ruler"). Early archaeological explorations at Thessalonica discovered an official stone inscription adjacent to the Vardar Gate on the west side of the city which specified "politarchs" as the leaders of the city in the 1st century AD. Subsequent discoveries and research demonstrated that the position of politarch was an annual magistracy in use by the free cities of Macedonia Province starting in the Roman period, and there were multiple politarchs in office at once rather than a single ruler.

The majority of the recovered politarch inscriptions have been discovered in Thessalonica, indicating the continuous use and prominence of this particular position in Thessalonica and around Macedonia from the 1st century BC to the 3rd century AD. In fact, one politarch recorded on a 1st-century AD inscription from Thessalonica was Aristarchus, who shares the same uncommon name, time period, and citizenship as "Aristarchus, a Macedonian of Thessalonica" who also became a Christian and friend of Paul, suggesting the possibility that the Aristarchus mentioned in Acts may also have been noted in a 1st-century inscription from Thessalonica.

By the time the apostle Paul arrived in about AD 49, Thessalonica was the capital and most important city of Macedonia Province. As was mentioned in the previous section, Paul followed his regular protocol and reasoned from the Scriptures in the synagogue for three Sabbaths, which resulted in some of the Jews, many of the God-fearers, and even certain women of the elite becoming Christians.

However, those who were unpersuaded formed a mob and accused Paul and the Christians of sedition, stating that he was upsetting the Empire, breaking the decrees of Caesar, and swearing allegiance to another king. Because Paul and his team could not be immediately found, the mob instead brought Jason and other local Christians before the politarchs. There was no legal authority to prosecute on the basis of a religious dispute, but a bond or fine was paid before their release, and Paul was obligated to leave the city, presumably by order of these politarchs, in order to avoid a riot.

> *They began dragging Jason and some brethren before the city authorities [politarchs] (Acts 17:6).*

(90) Altar to the Unknown God
(Unknown Gods Altars)

Date: 1st century BC

Discovered: Palatine Hill, Rome

Period: Apostles and the Early Church

Keywords: Athens; altar; Areopagus; Rome

Bible Passage: Acts 17:22-34

Found at Pergamum, Miletus, and Phrygia, altars of the Roman period have been discovered with Greek inscriptions stating dedication to "unknown gods." A 1st-century BC altar found on the Palatine Hill in Rome inscribed in Latin also mentions "whether to a god or goddess sacred" and has been compared to the "unknown god" altar of Athens. Allegedly, an altar to an unknown god was discovered in Athens in AD 1208 by Pope Innocent III, but it has not been located in modern times.

The concept of an altar to the unknown god has generated discussion, research, and debate due to its peculiarity and the way in which the apostle Paul used the inscription during his speech in Athens. At the Areopagus of Athens in about AD 50, Paul used an altar "to an unknown god" as an illustration to argue that the God called unknown to the Athenians is the one true God.

Ancient Greek philosophers used the generic *theos* (god) in their works to refer to an ambiguous supreme god, so Paul's explanation would have been particularly relevant to the educated philosophers of Athens that he addressed.

There was also important historical context for Athens. The altar to the unknown god may have been a result of the Cylon affair of the 6th century BC involving appeasement of an unknown god to abate a plague in Athens, and the proposed solution by Epimenides to sacrifice and make altars to the "unknown god."

A few writers of the Roman period, including the 2nd-century AD traveler and historian Pausanias, whose documentation is regarded as accurate, specifically mention the presence of altars dedicated to unknown gods, and even an unknown god.

Ancient sources and recently rediscovered altars confirm that the inscribed "unknown god" altar that Paul made reference to in Athens was an actual monument and not merely a hypothetical object used for a speech.

> *While I was passing through and examining the objects of your worship, I also found an altar with this inscription, "TO AN UNKNOWN GOD" (Acts 17:23).*

(91) The Corinth Synagogue
(Synagogue of the Hebrews Inscription)

Date: 4th century AD

Discovered: Corinth, Greece

Period: Apostles and the Early Church

Keywords: Corinth; synagogue

Bible Passage: Acts 18:1-8

When Paul moved to Corinth about AD 50, he began teaching in the synagogue there as was his normal protocol. Archaeological excavations at the ancient city of Corinth uncovered a Greek inscription, perhaps a sign, reading "synagogue of the Hebrews" and a decorative stone depicting three menorah motifs, representing the menorah originally in the Jerusalem temple and often used as artwork in ancient synagogues.

Based on the location of the discovery of the synagogue inscription, the synagogue at Corinth was probably near the forum, north of the Peirene Fountain, and along a main street called the Lechaion Road, which went north-south through the city.

Philo of Alexandria, a Jewish philosopher, also made reference to a substantial community of Jews in Corinth in his 1st-century AD work about a diplomatic mission to Emperor Caligula.

Although the Corinth synagogue inscription probably dates to the 4th century AD, most synagogues in the ancient world were constructed directly over earlier synagogue remains when being repaired or rebuilt, so the synagogue at Corinth in use during the 1st century and the time of Paul was probably at the same location. The synagogue of the Hebrews sign and the decorative menorah stone confirm the existence of a synagogue in Corinth during the Roman period, and point to its location on the north side of the city near the forum.

> *Crispus, the leader of the synagogue, believed in the Lord with all his household, and many of the Corinthians when they heard were believing and being baptized (Acts 18:8).*

(92) Gallio the Governor
(Delphi Inscription)

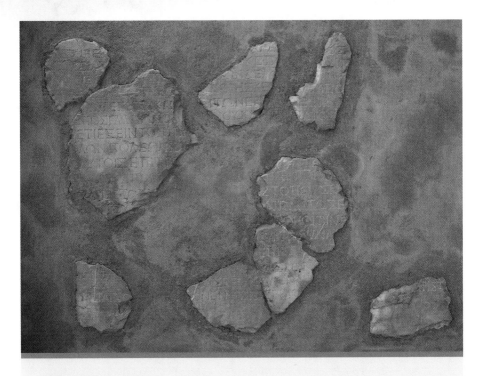

Date: AD 52

Discovered: Delphi, Greece

Period: Apostles and the Early Church

Keywords: Gallio; Corinth; governor; Delphi; Claudius; Achaia

Bible Passage: Acts 18:12-17

After Paul had lived for a year and a half in Corinth, the capital of Achaia province, Jews who opposed the message he was teaching brought him before the judgment seat and the Roman proconsul in about AD 51.[116] Standing before this proconsul at the judgment seat, or *bema*, located in the south side of the forum, many of the Jews in Corinth thought that Paul might be prosecuted and that they would soon be rid of him.[117] The book of Acts identifies this proconsul, or governor, as a man named Gallio who seemed disinterested in listening to the religious charges or judging Paul.

At Delphi, located north of Corinth in Achaia province, excavations around the temple of Apollo uncovered an official Roman inscription that records an edict of Emperor Claudius from about AD 52 in Greek. Carved into limestone and represented by nine known fragments, the edict gives an order to invite citizens to replenish the depopulated city of Delphi, names the emperor as Claudius in his twelfth year, and states that the proconsul or governor of the province of Achaia at this time was a friend of the emperor named Junius Gallio.

This inscription demonstrates that Gallio served a term as proconsul of Achaia around AD 51–52, confirming the information recorded in Acts and providing a useful chronological detail that situates Paul in Corinth around AD 50–51. This Roman official had his official residence at Corinth where he encountered the apostle Paul and may have exercised what the Romans referred to as *cognition extra ordinem*, in which Gallio as judge could decline an accusation that he deemed extraordinary or irrelevant.

Gallio is also known from Roman writings of the 1st and 2nd centuries, such as Cassius Dio, Seneca, and Tacitus. In particular, the philosopher Seneca the Younger, brother of Gallio, indicates that Gallio left his position as proconsul in Achaia with a distaste for the area, which can also be seen in his apathetic behavior when Paul was accused in Corinth. Seneca later met a tragic fate when Nero executed him for allegedly participating in an assassination attempt as part of the Piso conspiracy, and Gallio was publicly denounced and probably committed suicide soon after.

> *While Gallio was proconsul of Achaia, the Jews with one accord rose up against Paul and brought him before the [bema] (Acts 18:12).*

---

[116] A proconsul was a governor of a Roman province who was under the jurisdiction of the Senate, in contrast to provinces controlled by the emperor.

[117] The platform on which Gallio stood or sat was about 7.5 feet above the stone pavement in the forum where the accused and onlookers stood. It was here that the proconsul would address citizens, settle disputes, or render verdicts on criminal cases. Paul used the *bema* in his letters to the Corinthians and Romans as a familiar word picture to communicate a teaching about the judgment seat of Christ (Romans 14:10-12; 2 Corinthians 5:10).

(93) Erastus of Corinth
(Erastus Pavement Inscription)

Date: AD 50

Discovered: Corinth, Greece

Period: Apostles and the Early Church

Keywords: Erastus; Corinth; treasurer

Bible Passages: Acts 19:21-22; Romans 16:23; 2 Timothy 4:20

In Acts and the epistles, both Luke and the apostle Paul often recorded the names and titles of people that Paul encountered during his missionary journeys, allowing readers and investigators to test and confirm the accuracy of the historical narrative.

When Paul moved to Corinth in about AD 50, many people throughout the city became Christians after listening to Paul persuasively preach the gospel and reason from the Scriptures. One of these was a man named Erastus who became a friend of Paul, and according to the book of Romans, this Erastus was the "manager of the city" or city "treasurer" of Corinth.

During excavations at Corinth in 1929, archaeologists found a rectangular pavement stone near the theatre with a Latin inscription mentioning Erastus. It translates as "Erastus in return for his aedileship paved it at his own expense," acknowledging the act of philanthropy and specifying the name and title of the official. This commemorative inscription specifically names Erastus and his title aedile, which was a city official chosen annually who managed public works and commercial affairs.[118] In the letter to the Romans, Paul used a Greek phrase equivalent to the Latin term aedile. The inscription from Corinth was dated to approximately AD 50, meaning it confirms the existence, occupation, time, and location of Erastus of Corinth, a Christian and friend of Paul who is mentioned in the books of Acts, Romans, and 2 Timothy.

Along with other ancient inscriptions attesting to Roman officials who were documented in Acts as becoming Christians, such as Sergius Paulus, the status of Erastus also demonstrates that the early church was composed of people from all economic and social classes in the Roman Empire.

Erastus, the city treasurer greets you (Romans 16:23).

---

[118] Another aedile inscription found in the forum of Corinth, dating to the reign of Emperor Augustus, states that a monument was erected at the expense of Babbius the aedile. These honorific inscriptions on stone could also be considered self-aggrandizement and may have been something Paul used as a contrasting example to spiritual matters, written with the Spirit of God on human hearts rather than stone slabs (2 Corinthians 3:1-3).

(94) ARTEMIS AND EPHESUS
(Statue of Artemis)

Date: 1st century AD

Discovered: Ephesus, Turkey

Period: Apostles and the Early Church

Keywords: Ephesus; Artemis; statue; idol; goddess; temple

Bible Passages: Acts 19:23-41; Ephesians 2:19-22; 2 Timothy 4:12-15

The temple of Artemis in Ephesus, originally built in the 8th century BC, was one of the largest, most impressive, and most revered temples in the ancient world, resulting in it also being named one of the wonders of the ancient world.

Inside the temple was the sacred cult statue of Artemis carved out of ebony, while in front of the temple and at other key locations were intricately carved marble statues of the goddess, including one from the 1st century AD that was discovered nearly intact and the size of a human. This particular statue had been carefully packed in dirt inside the Hestia sanctuary, perhaps to hide and preserve it, and it serves as an example of the statue that once stood in the temple of Artemis.

The known statues of Artemis are decorated with a zodiac necklace, animal figurines, and unidentified objects on the chest and stomach of the image, with various theories suggesting breasts, bull testicles, eggs, or fruits, but nearly all agree that they are representative of fertility.

However, Artemis was also known as a perpetually virgin goddess, and therefore her cult differed significantly from Aphrodite. Artemis was a mother goddess associated with virginity, fertility, magic, astrology, and hunting.

Inscriptions from Ephesus also describe Artemis as a savior and a goddess who was able to answer prayers. Animal bones have been discovered around the temple, indicating that sacrifices were made to her at the massive altar and the statue of the goddess located in the central courtyard of the temple.

The cult of Artemis in Ephesus had a powerful and ancient following, with followers so dedicated that religious life in Ephesus was unique.[119] Established more than 1,000 years before Paul arrived in Ephesus, the worship of Artemis was not one that could be ignored or easily overturned. Worship of the goddess was allegedly even more ancient than the Greek migration to the city of Ephesus, which was named after one of the founders.

According to archaeological findings, silversmiths associated with the cult of Artemis, mentioned by Luke, seem to have made silver shrines containing an image of Artemis, while small terracotta, silver, and gold images and statuettes of Artemis have also been found. As followers of Artemis and as craftsmen, the silversmiths saw a serious threat to their cult and their business if people continued to accept Christianity and reject the worship of Artemis. Years later, Paul wrote to the Ephesians that they were a temple of God, which would have been understood as a contrast to the temple of Artemis in their city.

> *Who does not know that the city of the Ephesians is guardian of the temple of the great goddess Artemis and of the image which fell from Zeus?* (Acts 19:35 AUTHOR'S TRANSLATION).

---

[119] The cult of Artemis had become so powerful and popular even outside of Ephesus that during the Roman period, there were at least 33 temples to Artemis in the Empire, and prominent generals and politicians often offered sacrifices at the temple. Although many other gods were worshipped at Ephesus, including deified emperors, she was by far the most important deity in the 1st century.

(95) TROUBLE AT THE JERUSALEM TEMPLE
(Temple Warning Inscription)

Date: 1st century AD

Discovered: Temple Mount, Jerusalem

Period: Apostles and the Early Church

Keywords: Jerusalem; temple; sign

Bible Passage: Acts 21:27-34

A rectangular stone, inscribed in the 1st century AD with a warning in Greek, was discovered in Jerusalem near the ruins of the Herodian temple complex in 1871.[120]

---

[120] The nearly intact stone block discovered in 1871 measures 33.5 centimeters long, 22.5 centimeters tall, and 14.5 centimeters deep. The fragment of a second stone sign discovered in 1936 contains part of six lines of the text.

The text of seven lines on the stone proclaims that any foreigner who enters the temple or the sacred space immediately around it could suffer the death penalty: "No foreigner is to go beyond the balustrade around the plaza of the temple area. Whoever is caught doing so will have himself to blame for his subsequent death." In 1936, a stone fragment of a second warning inscription with the same text was discovered near the Lion's Gate in Jerusalem.

According to the book of Acts, when Paul briefly returned to Jerusalem in AD 57, the main accusation of the Jews against Paul was that he brought Trophimus the Ephesian, a Greek and a foreigner, with him into the sacred area of the temple complex, thus defiling the holy place. This was a major offense according to the Law, and according to the warning signs in the 1st century, an action that might result in death. The writings of Josephus also mention the signs and the practice of this law around the time of Paul, prior to AD 70.

The two stone warning-inscription discoveries attest to the existence and enforcement of this particular custom and law during the 1st century AD and demonstrate the serious nature of the allegations against Paul. Although Paul was falsely accused of bringing a non-Israelite into the temple court, he nearly died for it and subsequently spent two years imprisoned in Caesarea because of the situation.

> "He has even brought Greeks into the temple and has defiled this holy place." For they had previously seen Trophimus the Ephesian in the city with him, and they supposed that Paul had brought him into the temple...and taking hold of Paul they dragged him out of the temple, and immediately the doors were shut. While they were seeking to kill him, a report came up to the commander of the Roman cohort that all Jerusalem was in confusion (Acts 21:27-31).

(96) JAMES, BROTHER OF JESUS
(James Ossuary)

Date: AD 62

Discovered: Unspecified tomb, Jerusalem

Period: Apostles and the Early Church

Keywords: James; martyr; ossuary; Jerusalem

Bible Passages: Matthew 13:55-56; Mark 6:3; Acts 21:17-18; Galatians 1:19; 2:9; James 1:1; Jude 1:1

© Paradiso. The James ossuary was on display at the Royal Ontario Museum from November 15, 2002 to January 5, 2003.

In Judea and Galilee and especially around Jerusalem from the 1st century BC to AD 70, the use of a carved stone box called an ossuary was popular in which the bones of deceased relatives were commonly stored and placed within a tomb. Nearly 1,000 ossuaries from this period have been found, and approximately 25 percent of those ossuaries have inscriptions. While many of these bone boxes were unfortunately looted from tombs rather than discovered in archaeological excavations, the artifacts can still provide valuable information when analyzed.

The "James Ossuary" had been acquired under mysterious circumstances and was in the possession of an antiquities collector in Israel before being revealed to the world in 2002. An expert in epigraphy examined the inscription on the side of the ossuary, which is in Aramaic and translates as "James son of Joseph brother of Jesus." Because of the names and their relationships to each other, the possible historical implications of the inscription made the artifact immediately famous and controversial.

Although this artifact was part of a forgery trial, after detailed analysis many scholars concluded that the ossuary and its inscription were authentic.[121] Analysis

---

[121] After the James Ossuary was put on display in Toronto, the Israeli government confiscated it under charges of forgery and illegal dealing in antiquities based on the evaluations of a team of scholars from the Israel Antiquities Authority.

showed that the ossuary, which measures 19.9 inches by 9.8 inches by 12.0 inches, was made of local Jerusalem limestone. The patina, or ancient residue, demonstrated that the ossuary had been inside a tomb in the Jerusalem area, and although the exact find location is not known with certainty, there is a probable tomb origin based on information about looted tombs in Jerusalem at the time when the ossuary first appeared. The craftsmanship of the artifact and the style of the letters also indicate an origin in 1st-century AD Jerusalem before AD 70.

James, the brother of Jesus, is mentioned in the Gospels, Acts, 1 Corinthians, Galatians, and Jude, and he wrote the Epistle of James. The writings of Josephus also record the martyrdom of James in Jerusalem in about AD 62 and state his family relationship to Jesus, meaning it is expected that the bones of James would have been placed in an ossuary prior to AD 70 in Jerusalem.

Several years of research demonstrate that the ossuary stone box itself is authentic and from a Jerusalem tomb used before AD 70; the Aramaic inscription is genuine and ancient; besides James the apostle there is no other known James, son of Joseph, brother of Jesus from this period; a statistical name analysis determined it was probable that only one person would have been described as "James son of Joseph brother of Jesus" in 1st-century AD Jerusalem; and of all the known inscribed ossuaries, only one other mentions a brother, meaning that the brother was very significant.

© Paradiso. The James ossuary was on display at the Royal Ontario Museum from November 15, 2002 to January 5, 2003.

All of this data indicates that the inscription refers to James the apostle and leader of the Jerusalem church, and to Jesus Christ, which makes it the only known 1st-century AD inscription mentioning either James or Jesus.

> *But I did not see any other of the apostles except James, the Lord's brother (Galatians 1:19).*

The James Ossuary became the centerpiece for an antiquities trial that involved many artifacts and lasted eight years, but in the end, the forgery charges were dropped and the artifacts were returned. The stone box and the inscription were authenticated by many scholars, but not by a complete consensus. While a group of scholars continued to claim that the inscription or part of the inscription was not authentic, many experts have agreed that it is a genuine 1st-century AD Aramaic inscription from Jerusalem mentioning a James, Joseph, and Jesus.

(97) Fighting Wild Beasts
(Bestiarius Oil Lamp)

Date: 1st century AD

Discovered: Unknown, Asia Province (western Turkey)

Period: Apostles and the Early Church

Keywords: bestiarius; persecution; Paul; lion; martyr; Ephesus

Bible Passages: 1 Corinthians 4:9; 15:32; 2 Corinthians 1:8-11; 6:5; 11:23; 2 Timothy 4:16-17

In the Roman Empire, a bestiarius was a person who went into arena combat against a powerful wild animal, either as a form of execution or a combat competition similar to gladiators. The animals were typically lions or bears that were hungry, angry, and ready to kill any human near them. According to Cicero, one such lion successfully dispatched 200 bestiarii.

When a person was condemned to death *ad bestias* as an enemy of the state, they were forced into the arena unarmed and often chained, with virtually no hope of survival, especially if multiple beasts were available to be sent against them. During times of persecution, many Christians in the Roman Empire were sentenced to death by beast as a spectacle in the arenas, probably beginning as early as the reign of Claudius.

A 1st-century AD oil lamp from Asia Province depicts a man, condemned *ad bestias*, being attacked by two lions. Similar artwork, including a marble relief, has also been discovered at Ephesus, and a wall painting depicting gladiators and lions in the arena was found in the theatre at Corinth.

During the more than two years of ministry in Ephesus, which is only briefly covered in Acts, Paul and the Christians probably encountered other obstructions and persecutions that were not recorded. It is even possible that Paul was condemned to battle wild animals in the arena. In his letter to the Corinthians, written from Ephesus, Paul stated that he "fought wild beasts at Ephesus," and that he and the apostles had been exhibited as men condemned to death, and as a "spectacle" to the world.

In his second letter to the church at Corinth, Paul wrote that in Asia Province he and the brethren despaired of life, but God delivered them from death. Later, in his second letter to Timothy, Paul stated that he was rescued out of the lion's mouth, although this may have been in reference to later events in Rome.

Several ancient church scholars considered the Corinthians passage to be referring to an actual battle with beasts, and early Christian apocryphal literature, such as the Acts of Paul and Acts of Titus, also recorded that Paul fought with beasts, and specifically a lion, in the stadium at Ephesus.

Many of the early Christians suffered such a fate, and Christian writers such as Tertullian and Cyprian described the practice as perverse, inhuman, and repulsive. Perhaps when Paul was in the Province of Asia around AD 52–55, and his enemies opposed his preaching and teaching, he was forced into the arena against a lion at the Ephesus stadium as a bestiarius, but he survived and carried on his mission.

If [according to man] I fought with wild beasts at Ephesus, what does it profit me? (1 Corinthians 15:32).

(98) PAUL ON MALTA
(First Man of Malta Inscription)

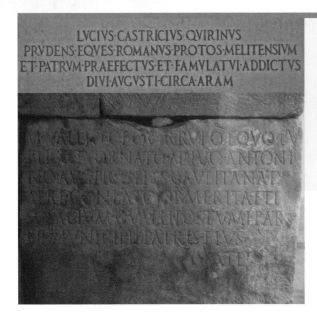

LVCIVS·CASTRICIVS·QVIRINVS
PRVDENS·EQVES·ROMANVS·PROTOS·MELITENSIVM
ET·PATRVM·PRAEFECTVS·ET·FAMVLATVI·ADDICTVS
DIVI·AVGVSTI·CIRCA·ARAM

Date: 2nd century AD

Discovered: Gozo, Malta

Period: Apostles and the Early Church

Keywords: Malta; Publius

Bible Passage: Acts 28:1-7

After being shipwrecked on the island of Malta, the apostle Paul was welcomed for three days at a nearby estate of a man named Publius who was referred to as "the first man of the island." This "first man" appears to have been a Roman political title used on Malta in the 1st century AD. A 1st-century AD Greek inscription from the reign of Emperor Tiberius honored Prudens, a Roman of equestrian rank who was called "the first of the Maltese" and "father," probably holding the same title and position as Publius did nearly 30 years later when Paul encountered him on the island near the end of AD 59.[122]

Another Greek inscription from the time of Tiberius also notes a Prudens who was "the first [man] of Malta and Gozo." The Romans had set up a local magistrate over the island, designated with the Latin title *municipi Melitesium primus omnium* ("the first over all in the municipality of Malta") according to another 1st-century

---

[122] A member of the equestrian rank, or knight, was a Roman aristocrat who owned substantial property and was able to hold military and political offices. The equites were below the senatorial class and above the plebeians and the proletariat.

AD inscription mentioning a temple of Apollo. Serving under the governor of Sicily, the Roman province to which Malta belonged at that time, Publius would have been the local leader of the island.

Beginning in the time of Augustus, and probably continuing through the 1st century AD, the ruler of this area presided over both Malta and the adjacent island of Gozo. Two similar Latin inscriptions of the 2nd century AD from Gozo honored Caius Vallius the "father of the municipality" during the reign of Hadrian prior to AD 138 but lacking the "first man" title, which appears to have been a higher position.

Inscriptions from the 1st and 2nd century AD from Malta and Gozo demonstrate that at the time of Paul, the Roman official presiding over the island of Malta was of the equestrian or knight rank and referred to using the title "first man" of the island Malta. The estate of Publius would have been in the architectural style of a Roman villa, belonging to a wealthy local man who apparently held a position of political prominence on the island.[123]

The church of St. Paul Milkghi (San Pawl Milqi), inland and not far from St. Paul's Bay, supposedly marks the location of the house of Publius according to tradition. Excavations did discover that a Roman villa was present on the site of the church, making the identification at least possible.

However, archaeologists also excavated and identified the mansion of the Roman governor of Malta at the outskirts of Rabat, the ancient capital. This house of the governor was in use during the reign of Claudius according to a statue of the emperor discovered there. This was also the time period when Paul was on Malta and Publius was the "first man" of Malta, suggesting that the house was the residence of Publius while Paul was shipwrecked on the island.

Around that place were lands belonging to the first man of the island, named Publius (Acts 28:7 AUTHOR'S TRANSLATION).

---

[123] Publius was a common praenomen (personal name) for Romans, used in circumstances of familiarity, which Luke employs often for the names of Christians in Acts, and this was probably the reason why Luke used his praenomen rather than the more formal cognomen. According to Jerome, Publius may have later become the bishop of Athens after Dionysus the Areopagite and was martyred.

(99) TITUS AND THE TEMPLE DESTRUCTION
(Arch of Titus Relief)

Date: AD 82

Discovered: Rome, Italy

Period: Apostles and the Early Church

Keywords: temple; menorah; triumph; Jerusalem; Rome; Titus; Domitian

Bible Passages: Numbers 8:4; 2 Chronicles 13:11; Luke 19:28-46; 21:5-6; 2 Corinthians 2:14

In AD 70, Jerusalem was destroyed by the Romans, and for this victory the general and future emperor Titus, along with his father Emperor Vespasian, received a triumph celebration in Rome, which is depicted on the Arch of Titus. In response to a revolt, the Romans under general Titus besieged Jerusalem, destroying the city and obliterating the temple.

In Jerusalem, toppled stones from the ruins of the temple complex were uncovered on an ancient street of the 1st century AD, next to remains of the western retaining wall of the Temple Mount where the stones had fallen from. The Arch of Titus in Rome, completed under Domitian in AD 82, depicts items looted from the Jerusalem temple after the destruction, including the gold menorah (lampstand), table of showbread, and trumpet, plus the triumphal entry of Titus into Rome.

The triumphal entry of Jesus into Jerusalem was a momentous event recorded by all four Gospel writers. The name of the event, derived from the Roman triumph celebration, is not found in the Gospels, although Paul appears to use the term in 1 Corinthians, but it is an appropriate description for a king entering his capital city during a procession of his subjects or followers.

In ancient Roman culture, a triumphant victor, known as *vir triumphalis* ("man of triumph") would enter the city in a celebration parade wearing the laurel wreath and a purple garment, which identified him with the royal and the divine, while riding in a chariot pulled by four horses, alluding to Sol the sun god. After entering the city, the victor would go to the temple of Jupiter and make a sacrifice in thanks to the gods.

In Rome, this procession would begin at the Campus Martius, outside the boundary of the city at the western bank of the Tiber River. Then the victor would enter the city through a triumphal gate, continue through the Circus Flaminius near the Capitoline Hill, go along the triumphal way toward the Circus Maximus, onto the Via Sacrum, into the Forum, and then to the temple of Jupiter on the Capitoline Hill where sacrifice was offered.

By the time of Jesus, the requirements and meaning of a triumphal entry had shifted slightly from its earlier roots associating it with a conquering hero, as it became even more significant and representative of kingship and divinity. In a comparable fashion, Jesus began His triumphal entry outside the boundaries of Jerusalem in Bethphage on the Mount of Olives, rode on a donkey like the kings of Israel, descended down the road into the Kidron Valley, entered the city through the Susa Gate, and went up to the temple where He cleansed it of merchants and moneychangers.

> *The days will come upon you when your enemies will throw up a barricade against you, and surround you and hem you in on every side, and they will level you to the ground and your children within you, and they will not leave in you one stone upon another, because you did not recognize the time of your visitation (Luke 19:43-44).*

(100) DOMITIAN AS A GOD
("Genius" of Emperor Domitian)

Date: AD 81–96

Discovered: Rome, Italy

Period: Apostles and the Early Church

Keywords: Domitian; John; Revelation; statue; idol

Bible Passages: Acts 17:7; 1 Timothy 6:13-16; Revelation 1:9; 17:9-18

Reigning as emperor of Rome from AD 81–96, Domitian, who was the son of Vespasian and brother of Titus, revived the Imperial cult and became known even among the Roman senators and patrician families as a despot with delusions of being a god.

A marble statue depicting the "genius" of Domitian, understood as his representative spirit or soul, demonstrates the idea of his divinity, which he promoted later in his reign. The figure, depicted with the cornucopia (or "horn of plenty" associated with numerous deities) and the aegis (animal skin with a gorgon head associated with deities, emperors, and heroes), was found near Via Labicana in Rome.

Usually a genius statue was representative of a group, such as the people of Rome, the Senate, or a particular family, yet the statue of the genius of Domitian, which essentially depicts the divine aspect of Domitian, can be compared to the "divine king" concept known and practiced in many ancient cultures.

Statues of the genius of a Roman emperor were extremely rare, perhaps only represented elsewhere with Augustus after his death, meaning the genius of Domitian statue made during his reign appears to be unique to Domitian. Other acts of Domitian, such as deifying his brother and other members of his family, building a temple of his family on the house where he was born, and insisting that he be addressed as *dominus et deus* ("lord and god"), demonstrate that he considered himself a living god whom the people should worship. Domitian also initiated, promoted, and hosted the games, including gladiatorial contests and beast fights, where he not only honored various deities, but also portrayed himself like a god.

As his reign continued, Domitian became increasingly despotic, and the Senate began to despise him. According to the Roman writers Martial, Pliny the Younger, Statius, and Suetonius, who were contemporary with Domitian, by AD 86 he required officials to address him as *dominus et deus* (lord and god), and Domitian was recognized as a totalitarian despot.

However, his self-deification and policy of worship and sacrifice to the emperor was resisted by many throughout the Empire, including Christians, which resulted in persecution. Polycarp and Tertullian of the 2nd century AD and Origen of the 3rd century AD remarked how Christians would have preferred death instead of following the requirement of emperor worship and making an oath by the genius of the emperor, while the 2nd-century AD Acts of John, Tertullian, and the 4th-century AD historian Eusebius record persecution of Christians during the reign of Domitian.

Because of his preaching of the gospel, teaching of the Bible, opposition to the imperial cult and emperor worship, and his status as a church leader and last surviving apostle, John was taken to Rome from Ephesus by order of Emperor Domitian. According to Tertullian, who lived only decades after, John was plunged into boiling oil, perhaps before an audience at the Colosseum or Circus Maximus. However, John survived this ordeal, so in AD 94, the fourteenth year of the reign of Domitian, he was banished to the remote island of Patmos, which was a punishment utilized by the Romans for political and religious prisoners of great influence, and a method that Domitian specifically is known to have used. According to Eusebius and Cassius Dio, Domitian exiled Flavia Domitilla for Christianity, along with her husband the Roman consul Flavius Clemens.

It was on the island of Patmos that John received the visions and wrote the book of Revelation before being allowed to return to Ephesus in AD 96, after Domitian was assassinated, Nerva was appointed the new emperor of Rome, and many were pardoned.

> *I, John, your brother and fellow partaker in the tribulation and kingdom and perseverance which are in Jesus, was on the island called Patmos because of the word of God and the testimony of Jesus (Revelation 1:9).*

(101) EARLY NEW TESTAMENT MANUSCRIPTS
(John Rylands Papyrus 52)

Date: AD 100–200

Discovered: Egypt

Period: Apostles and the Early Church

Keywords: Bible; Gospel; manuscript; codex

Bible Passages: John 18:31-33,37-38; 1 Peter 1:22-25

Of all the writings from antiquity still in existence today, the New Testament is by far the best represented in terms of the number of ancient manuscripts and their quality. Most ancient documents are known only from a few copies dating to centuries after their original composition, but not only do ancient copies of the books and letters of the New Testament number in the hundreds, but at least 15 of these manuscript fragments date to within 150 years of the original composition, with a few being only decades removed from when the autograph was written.[124]

Perhaps the earliest known of the New Testament fragments is a piece of papyrus roughly triangular in shape, about 3.5 inches long (8.9 cm) and 2.5 inches wide (6 cm), with 7 lines of Greek writing in black ink on both sides, totaling 118 legible letters and containing John 18:31-33,37-38.[125] This piece of papyrus was originally

---

[124] An *autograph* of an ancient manuscript is the original work. For the Gospel of John, this would have been the scroll (or possibly codex) on which John the apostle first wrote his Gospel account, perhaps around AD 62–66 in Ephesus. Many scholars argue for a composition date of the Gospel of John around AD 90, but John makes no mention of the AD 70 destruction of the temple and Jerusalem, the present existence of the pool of Bethesda, no allusion to the revolt of the Jews against the Romans in AD 66, and John 21:18-23 may indicate that the martyrdom of Peter in AD 64 had not yet occurred.

[125] Or approximately 9 cm by 6 cm, originally part of a page about 22 cm tall and 20 cm wide.

part of a codex, or book, which became a popular format for collections of Christian writings beginning in the 1st century AD rather than a more cumbersome scroll.[126]

This specific section of John contains part of the trial of Jesus before Pontius Pilate at the Praetorium in Jerusalem and is therefore extremely significant historically. Designated P52 (Papyrus 52) and part of the John Rylands Library collection, the fragment was acquired from Egypt in 1920, demonstrating that the Gospel of John had been copied and circulated widely in the Roman Empire after only a few decades.[127]

---

[126] A significant contribution to the circulation and spread of the New Testament was the codex. A codex is a collection of sheets of any material containing handwriting, folded and fastened at the spine, and usually protected by covers. The codex came into major use during the 1st century AD and seems to be referred to for writing an epistle in the New Testament on sheets of parchment (2 Timothy 4:13). The Roman poet Martial, in ca. AD 84, referred to the use of parchment for the codex as a vast improvement over the roll or scroll, and he circulated his works in codex form. The earliest copies of New Testament books are found almost exclusively in codex form, which was approximately 40 percent less expensive than scrolls, superior for transport and storage and better preservation, and easier to use because a codex has an additional advantage of pagination.

[127] Also designated as Greek Papyrus 457.

The date of this manuscript fragment has typically been placed around AD 100, with a range of about AD 90–200, and the clearest paleographic comparisons argued to be a manuscript of the *Iliad* dated to the end of the 1st century AD and a personal letter found in Egypt dated to AD 94. Although recently a few scholars have attempted to argue for a later date of the P52 fragment, the closest comparisons still indicate that it was copied around AD 100.

Due to the content, format, location, and date, P52 is extremely significant in demonstrating the early composition, copying, and circulation of the New Testament and the Gospel of John in particular.[128]

> *The grass withers,*
> *And the flower falls off,*
> *But the word of the Lord endures forever*
> *(1 Peter 1:24-25).*

---

[128] Another important early New Testament manuscript, Papyrus 46 (P46), contains the remains of an ancient Greek codex of the New Testament epistles of Romans, 1 Corinthians, 2 Corinthians, Ephesians, Galatians, Philippians, Colossians, 1 Thessalonians, and Hebrews. In antiquity, the codex probably also included the epistles of 2 Thessalonians and Philemon, and possibly other Pauline letters, but the final 7 leaves are missing. Originally numbering 104 leaves and measuring approximately 28 cm tall by 16 cm wide, text was written in black ink on both the front and back of the leaves, amounting to 205 pages. Today, 86 leaves of the original 104 are known. P46 was probably produced around AD 150, although a few scholars estimate a date of AD 225, but the codex represents the earliest known manuscript copies of the Pauline epistles. Paul wrote 2 Corinthians from Macedonia, probably at Philippi or Thessalonica in about AD 56, which means P46 is a copy possibly only around 95 years removed from the original composition. The top of each page has a designated number, using standard and archaic Greek letters for the numbering system, and each epistle has its title written and centered, such as "To the Corinthians 2." The text also uses *nomina sacra* (abbreviations of "sacred names") and other word abbreviations, plus a few corrections of missing or misspelled words that inevitably happen during the process of hand copying a long manuscript. Discovered about 1931 in the Fayoum region of Egypt in the ruins of an ancient church where it had been preserved for centuries, along with P45 and P47, the manuscript was taken to Cairo and sold. The codex is currently divided into two parts, and a few sections are missing.

CONCLUSION

Through the artifacts presented, a window to the ancient times of the Bible was opened, providing both context and evidence for those historical periods. Archaeological excavations and surveys have revealed houses, tombs, temples, palaces, and even whole cities, while the artifacts discovered often supply us with the additional information needed to construct a clearer and more thorough historical picture of the ancient past.

Although a comprehensive understanding of the past requires a synthesis of ancient histories, architecture, geography, and artifacts, the knowledge gained from artifacts can provide us with a valuable historical framework and additional insights unavailable from other forms of archaeological remains. Because artifacts also originate from all points of the social, economic, cultural, and religious spectrum, they give us perspectives from kings to peasants and from high priests to heretics.

Although archaeological artifacts do provide physical evidence for ancient written history, including the Bible, skepticism or dismissal of the Bible and the writings of the ancients is currently the dominant perspective in academia. While ancient texts such as the Bible or the *Annals of Thutmose III* or *History of the Peloponnesian War* or *The Twelve Caesars* are extremely useful for reconstructing history, critics often claim that these writings are biased propaganda that reflect the subjective opinions and agendas of the authors rather than objective retelling of the facts.

Artifacts, however, cannot be so easily dismissed or explained away as propaganda or mythology, since they are physical objects that were made at the time of the person, place, event, or practice and survived the centuries or even millennia without editing or changes.

Beginning in the 1800s, a skeptical viewpoint of the Bible known as higher criticism developed and became popularized, claiming that many of the people, places, and events of the Bible were simply myths or fairy tales developed to advance a religious and political agenda. Because very little physical evidence connected to the Bible had been discovered at that time, these claims were based on the absence of evidence argument and depended on ignorance or insufficient data.

The rise and adoption of this skeptical view, however, led to many scholars realizing the importance of physical evidence in establishing the historical reliability of the Bible and understanding its ancient context. Most artifacts connected to the Bible have been discovered during official excavations of sites in the Middle East and the Mediterranean region, but many important artifacts have also been illegally excavated, looted, or were undocumented. These "unprovenanced" finds usually turned up on the antiquities market and were sold to museums or collectors, which in turn were occasionally resold or donated.

Although the illegally acquired artifacts lack details of context and documentation, many have been of historical importance and should be verified and studied. The majority of the significant artifacts, both from official excavations and the antiquities market, have made their way to museums and antiquities collections around the world, where the public can view them and scholars can study them.

The artifacts connected to the Bible span thousands of years stretching from the book of Genesis to Revelation, with discoveries that relate directly, such as the record of a specific event that is also recorded in the Bible, and indirectly, informing the context during a certain period of biblical history. As the remnants of the past, these artifacts give essential firsthand insight and accounts of history from thousands of years ago. Without these artifacts, many passages of the Bible would not be correctly understood or would be open to historical attacks by sceptics of the Bible.

Artifacts related to the Bible specifically have illuminated or confirmed events, chronologies, practices, terminology, locations, and individuals that would otherwise have remained a mystery. As an example, there are currently about 70 individuals mentioned in the Old Testament who have been confirmed by archaeological artifacts, and about 32 individuals in the New Testament so far confirmed by archaeology, with several more people from the Bible tentatively identified by archaeological artifacts. Many artifacts have also illuminated obscure words and practices in the Bible, from times long ago in lands far away, that would be misunderstood or unknown otherwise.

In spite of this evidence from archaeology, in the academic world and the general public, the Bible is still typically viewed as a source of little or no historical value. Ancient cultures indeed mixed in their theological views and beliefs with their historical texts, just as is done in the modern era, often making outlandish statements and at times even obviously bending the historical record to make their nation look superior.

Yet, this is not true for every ancient document. Historical sections from the Bible often display the opposite and more objective tendency by recording failures, embarrassments, and defeats. Further, archaeology, and artifacts in particular, have confirmed the accuracy of many biblical passages. Because these artifacts can be traced to a specific region, city, or even building, and the objects can be dated to a point in time, they are among the most precise, accurate, and useful sources of information.

Without the details of time and location associated with certain artifacts, one could only suggest general similarities. Specificity is required, and therefore archaeological and historical attestation of passages in the Bible can only be suggested when thorough research has been conducted on these artifacts. The result of analysis of the artifacts and comparison to the relevant historical passages in the Bible, however, demonstrates accuracy in details of people, places, times, events, and practices.

If these discoveries remained buried and unknown, the tangible archaeological evidence for the historical reliability of the Bible would be restricted to ancient manuscripts and the ruins of buildings. Yet, we now have hundreds of significant artifacts that illuminate the ancient world of the Bible and demonstrate the historical accuracy of many passages.

In writing *Unearthing the Bible*, I chose an assortment of the most important and interesting artifacts that not only contextualized various time periods of biblical history, but also demonstrated that archaeological remains are connected to and provide historical support for the books of the Bible ranging from Genesis to Revelation, covering over 3,000 years of history with artifacts from multiple regions of the ancient world. And the degree of historical corroboration between the Bible and the artifacts that have been discovered over the last 150 years is startling, surpassing previous expectations and estimates, and continuing to astonish.

The fallacious arguments claiming that the archaeological data shows the Bible to be unhistorical myth, legend, or propaganda are demonstrated to be sensationalism and falsehood by the artifact evidence presented in this book. Although 101 objects were presented, there might have been around 500 artifacts noted if there were no space restrictions and the scope was more comprehensive!

Further, every year new and significant discoveries connected to the Bible are being made, suggesting that the amount of archaeological evidence will increase as time goes on and as ancient sites are found and excavated. Pass on this information to others, visit archaeological sites and museums to see these artifacts with your own eyes, and be on the lookout for these new exciting finds, which are usually announced in press releases, archaeology journals, and documentaries. Only time will tell what else lies buried, and the mysteries that will be revealed as more artifacts of the past are rediscovered.

KEY TERMS

Akkadian: Refers to the Akkadian language of Mesopotamia, the oldest known Semitic language, or to the empire or people from the Akkadian Empire, founded by Sargon of Akkad in the 24th century BC.

Antediluvian: Before the great flood.

Bulla/bullae: A lump of clay molded around a cord and stamped with a seal.

Cuneiform: A wedge-shaped form of writing invented by the Sumerians that was simplified from the pictographic writing system that preceded it. It was used to write numerous languages, including Sumerian, Akkadian, Hittite, and Eblaite.

Hieroglyphics: Any form of writing that uses pictures to represent letters or sounds. The most famous hieroglyphic writing system of the ancient world was used in Egypt.

Levant: A region of the Middle East including modern Syria, Jordan, Lebanon, Israel, and the Palestinian Territories.

Marduk: Patron god of Babylon and chief god of the pantheon by the 18th century BC. Marduk was also referred to by the title Bel. He was associated with the dragon.

Nomarch: The ruler or governor of a nome, or province, within ancient Egypt.

Obelisk: A tall monument with four sides and a tapering top that was usually carved out of stone and contained writing and illustrations.

Ossuary: A box, usually carved from stone, that stored human bones and was placed in a tomb.

Ostracon/ostraca: A pottery sherd containing writing, usually written using black carbon ink or inscribed into the piece of pottery.

Papyrus/Papyri: An early writing material similar to paper, made from the papyrus plant.

Petroglyphs: Images or writing carved into a large rock surface.

Prism: In archaeology, a prism typically refers to a four-sided clay artifact that usually contains writing on each of the sides.

Scarab: In ancient Egypt, small amulets or seals in the shape of the scarab beetle were carved out of stone or made from faience, and often inscribed with the name of a king or official in Egyptian hieroglyphs.

Semite: A designation referring to people of the ancient world who spoke a Semitic language, including Akkadian, Ammonite, Aramaic, Assyrian, Babylonian, Canaanite, Edomite, Hebrew, Moabite, Phoenician, and Ugaritic. The ancient Egyptians often referred to all people from western Asia as "Asiatics."

Stele: A monument stone or wooden slab erected for commemorative purposes, usually inscribed with writing and decoration, but occasionally painted.

Tablet: The clay tablets commonly used during the Bronze Age in the ancient Near East were typically rectangular in shape and the written text was impressed into the wet clay with a reed stylus. Some tablets were baked, others were dried, but many of the preserved tablets discovered by archaeologists underwent an unintentional hardening process when a building housing tablets was destroyed by fire.

Tell or Tel: A mound consisting of debris and ruins from ancient cities or towns built on top of one another at the same archaeological site. In certain situations, the mound was formed purposefully in order to create an artificial hill.

Ziggurat: A monumental structure of successively terraced platforms constructed with clay bricks. A ziggurat was associated with religion, usually had a shrine or temple at the top, and may have been seen as a connection between earth and the heavens. The Etemenanki ziggurat in Babylon, now in ruins, was approximately 300 feet tall (91 m), but larger ziggurats may have existed previously.

Archaeological Periods

Early Bronze I . . . . 3200–3000 BC

Early Bronze II . . . . 3000–2700 BC

Early Bronze III . . . . 2700–2200 BC

Intermediate Bronze Age . . . . 2200–2000 BC

Middle Bronze I . . . . 2000–1750 BC

Middle Bronze II . . . . 1750–1650 BC

Middle Bronze III . . . . 1650–1500 BC

Late Bronze I . . . . 1500–1400 BC

Late Bronze II . . . . 1400–1300 BC

Late Bronze IIB . . . . 1300–1200 BC

Iron IA . . . . 1200–1150 BC

Iron IB . . . . 1150–1000 BC

Iron IIA . . . . 1000–925 BC

Iron IIB . . . . 925–722 BC

Iron IIC . . . . 722–587 BC

Babylonian Period . . . . 587–539 BC

Persian Period . . . . 539–332 BC

Hellenistic Period . . . . 332–63 BC

Roman Period . . . . 63 BC–AD 325

TIMELINE

꒒꒒꒒

3298 BC   The end of the Flood, followed by the Tower of Babel (Genesis 7:1-10; 11:1-9)

3100 BC   Sumerian civilization (Genesis 10:10)

3000 BC   Egyptian Kingdom

2600 BC   Rise of Harrapan civilization in India

2400 BC   Akkadian civilization

1950 BC   The fall of Ur to the Elamites (Genesis 11:31)

1900 BC   Minoan civilization palace period on Crete

1876 BC   Promise given to Abraham (Genesis 17:1-8)

1750 BC   Code of Hammurabi

1707 BC   Joseph enters Egypt (Genesis 37:28,36)

1614 BC   Joseph dies (Genesis 50:22-26)

1570 BC   Pharaoh Ahmose I expels Hyksos, enslavement begins (Exodus 1:8-11)

1526 BC   Moses born (Exodus 2:1-10)

1446 BC   Exodus and Law of Moses (Exodus 20:1-26)

1404 BC   Israelites under Joshua begin the conquest (Joshua 1:1-6)

1260 BC   Pharaoh Rameses II treaty with the Hittites

1180 BC   Sea Peoples/Philistines invade Egypt and go to Canaan (Judges 10:6-7)

1010 BC   David begins his reign (2 Samuel 5:1-5)

967 BC   Fourth year of Solomon's reign; temple of Yahweh built (1 Kings 6:1)

931 BC   Kingdom splits into Israel and Judah (1 Kings 12:1-20)

926 BC   Shoshenq I (Shishak) invades Israel and Judah (2 Chronicles 12:1-9)

722 BC   Northern kingdom of Israel falls to Assyria (2 Kings 17:1-20)

701 BC   Sennacherib besieges Jerusalem (2 Kings 18:13–19:37)

587 BC   Kingdom of Judah destroyed by Nebuchadnezzar and Babylonians (2 Kings 25:1-21)

539 BC   Persians conquer Babylon and King Cyrus frees exiles (Daniel 5:30-31)

517 BC   Jerusalem temple rebuilt under Zerubbabel (Ezra 6:13-18)

479 BC   Esther made queen (Esther 2:1-18)

444 BC   Decree to rebuild Jerusalem walls under Nehemiah (Nehemiah 2:1-9)

332 BC   Alexander enters Jerusalem (Daniel 8:1-22)

63 BC   Pompey the Great conquers Jerusalem for the Roman Republic

40 BC   Herod the Great becomes king of Judea (Matthew 2:1)

27 BC   Octavian becomes Emperor Augustus (Luke 2:1)

8 BC   Census of Caesar Augustus (Luke 2:1-3)

8 BC   John the Baptizer born (Luke 1:57-66)

8 BC   Jesus of Nazareth born (Luke 2:4-21)

4 BC   Herod dies and leaves kingdom to Archelaus, Antipas, Philip, Salome (Matthew 2:19-23)

AD 6   Archelaus exiled and Judea becomes a province of the Empire (Matthew 2:22)

AD 12   Tiberius receives power as emperor (Luke 3:1)

AD 33   Jesus of Nazareth crucifixion and resurrection (Luke 23:20–24:12)

AD 34   Stephen martyred in Jerusalem (Acts 7:54-60)

AD 35   Paul of Tarsus conversion (Acts 9:1-22)

AD 41   Claudius becomes emperor and Nazareth Inscription Edict(Acts 18:2)

AD 44   Death of Herod Agrippa I (Acts 12:19-23)

AD 46   Paul to Cyprus and meeting with Sergius Paulus (Acts 13:4-12)

AD 47   Paul travels to Asia Minor (Acts 13:13–14:28)

AD 48   Jerusalem Council (Acts 15:1-33)

AD 49   Paul travels to Macedonia and Achaia (Acts 16:6–18:22)

AD 53   Paul in Ephesus (Acts 19:1–20:1)

AD 57   Paul taken to Caesarea Maritima (Acts 23:23–26:32)

AD 59   Shipwreck on Malta (Acts 28:1-11)

AD 60   Paul arrives in Rome (Acts 28:11-31)

AD 62   Paul released and final journeys

AD 62   James martyred in Jerusalem

AD 64   Great fire of Rome and Peter crucified (John 21:15-19)

AD 67   Paul of Tarsus beheaded in Rome (2 Timothy 4:6-8)

AD 70   Jerusalem destroyed (Luke 19:41-44)

AD 95   John writes Revelation on the island of Patmos (Revelation 1:1-3,9-11)

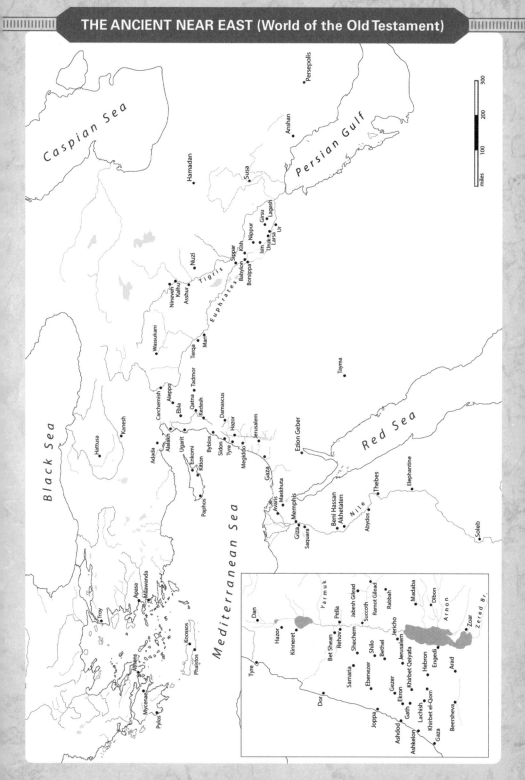

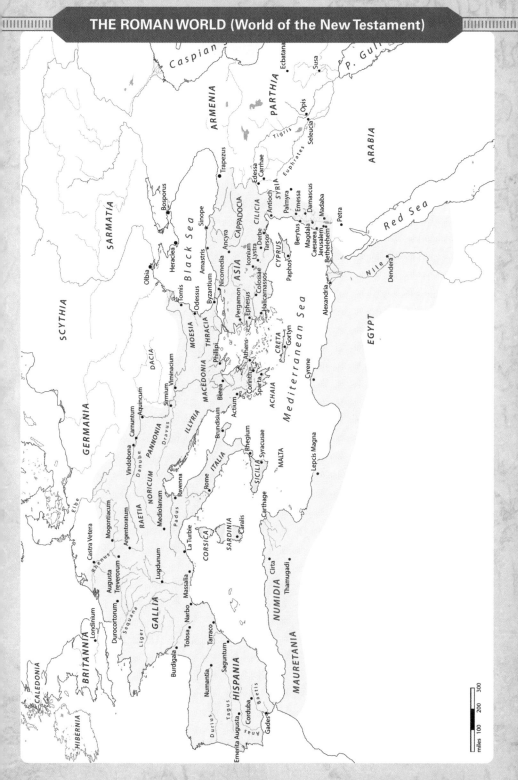

Scripture Index

Each Scripture citation in this index appears on
the opening page for an artifact in the book.

To learn more about Harvest House books and
to read sample chapters, visit our website:

www.harvesthousepublishers.com

HARVEST HOUSE PUBLISHERS
EUGENE, OREGON